To Dearest

With fon much love & affection

Heather x

CW01020381

MANY FACETS OF LOVE

Heather Lealan

ATHENA PRESS
LONDON

MANY FACETS OF LOVE
Copyright © Heather Lealan 2004

ISBN 1 84401 254 9

First Published 2004 by
ATHENA PRESS
Queen's House, 2 Holly Road
Twickenham, TW1 4EG
United Kingdom

Printed for Athena Press

MANY FACETS OF LOVE

This book is dedicated to
PAMELA PLUMMER
17th December 1935 - 17th August 1996
my spiritual teacher and friend
with gratitude and thanks
for the richness
she gave to
my life

Contents

Introduction

QUITE WHEN I BECAME AWARE OF THE HEALING ENERGY, coming from my hands, I am not exactly sure. But it happened about twelve years ago when I was in the middle of my aromatherapy/reflexology training. At first it was rather disconcerting, because I didn't have any understanding of what was happening to me. I believed that only members of the clergy were allowed to do this type of healing work. I have always believed in Jesus, and frequently prayed for guidance and advice, so I decided to ask him about this. After I had finished my prayer, I thought I'd go and do the washing up, and wait. I knew I'd get an answer sooner or later. It was to be sooner. I didn't get as far as the kitchen. Instead I found myself dusting off the Bible on the bookshelf. I'm not really into reading the Bible, so this was an unusual event for me. However, I opened it randomly. My eyes fell upon a scripture where the disciples asked Jesus how it was that he had the power of healing. He replied that they all had the power of healing, and that he would teach them, and then he wanted them to go out and teach all others. He didn't say just men or priests, but all others. I can't tell you where it is in the Bible. I didn't think of writing it down at the time. But from the moment I read that scripture, a wonderful feeling of elation and peace came over me. I knew that I had been given permission to heal. I also knew that we should also pass on our knowledge to each other.

I realise that there may be some who will question the authenticity of my answer, but I am convinced that I have been given permission to do healing work by the highest authority, and that is good enough for me.

It wasn't to be long before my healing training would start properly; within a few days in fact. I only went to the shop to buy a loaf of bread, and whilst in the queue waiting to be served, I could see a small A5 poster, glowing on the wall, next to me.

Naturally it caught my eye. It was advertising a healing centre that had just started. I didn't have a pen on me, so I memorised the phone number, and wrote it down as soon as I got home. I'll give them a ring later I thought, but all day a voice in my head kept saying, the number is wrong, you will have to put a two after the first digit. Of course, I ignored the advice when I came to ring the number that I had written down. Sure enough it was the wrong number. Perhaps I had remembered it wrongly I thought, so I tried again. This time I put the two in, as the voice in my head had suggested. I couldn't believe it. Not only was it the correct number, but the woman I spoke to was surprised that I had got through at all, because they realised after a lot of posters had gone out, that the phone number had been printed wrongly, and they were having to have some new ones printed.

My spiritual journey had just begun in earnest. In a few more days, I would meet Pam, my spiritual healing teacher, who would set me out along the path of a fascinating journey. A journey that would change my life and me, beyond recognition, giving me richness that I cannot describe in a few words. The journey so far, has seen me breaking down barriers, and old worn-out belief systems. It has filled me with wonder and awe, yet sometimes with confusion and frustration. It has sometimes left me feeling fearful for my sanity, and yet it has also filled me with a feeling of great honour and privilege. There have been times when I felt I should abandon the whole thing, and other times when my thirst for knowledge and truth, could not be quenched fast enough.

Whatever I have felt along the way, there is no going back. I have been privileged to so much information, knowledge and experience, in such a short space of time, that I can only count myself as lucky beyond measure.

I know that there is still yet much more to learn and understand about our vast universe. But what I have learned so far, I would like to share with you. The knowledge that I have gained along the way has come to me in different ways. I have read a vast amount of books, and have had many personal experiences of a spiritual and psychic nature. At times my spiritual guides have had me sit down, and have dictated information to me, via telepathy, from the spirit world. Pam, my spiritual teacher, gave me a great many gifts, as she taught me. One of those gifts was to show me how to recognise 'the wheat from the chaff'. I have been taught how to recognise the true and the false. So that I might not be fooled, by a lot of so called 'spiritual' rubbish and thus led up the garden path, away from the truth, I question and examine everything I read and experience very thoroughly.

This is why it has taken me nearly five years to write this book. Nothing has been written without much thought and prayer, nothing has been written in a hurry. I have been determined that this book should reflect the truth. I have done my utmost, to make sure that, in no way, are you misled or misinformed. To the best of my knowledge and the best of my ability, everything I have written in this book is the truth.

It has never been my intention, to try and prove to you that these things are true, but rather to share with you, the knowledge that I have been privileged to gain. If by so doing, some of your questions have been answered, your mind put at rest, or you have gained more insight and a better understanding of things, then this book will have done its job.

I hope you enjoy the book, as much as I have enjoyed writing it for you.

Chapter One

WHAT HAPPENS AFTER WE DIE?

ONE OF THE VERY LAST LESSONS MY SPIRITUAL TEACHER AND very dear friend gave to me happened on the day of her funeral. I've always believed we live on after death. There was no doubt in my mind at all. I've seen spirit people before, and I have no problem with that. But this day was different. I'd met Pam four years earlier, at a healing centre, where I had gone to offer my services free of charge as a reflexologist, in exchange for some help and guidance on how to deal with 'this healing stuff that was coming through my hands' as I put it to her when we first met. I knew immediately she was going to be my teacher of healing, and, more besides, as I confidently told her. She just smiled one of her knowing smiles, as she acknowledged what I had said with a simple 'that's right'.

In no time at all Pam had taken me under her wing, giving me group lessons and private lessons about Healing, Spirituality, Love and so many other wonderful things at her home. During this time our friendship also grew, and so it was with great sadness that I learned of her sudden death.

Now here I was at my friend's funeral, my husband at my side, on a beautiful sunny day, singing *All Things Bright and Beautiful*. Like me, Pam doesn't believe in morbid black funerals, so I was wearing a cream dress. Most of her friends were also wearing pastel shades, just as Pam had requested, a relaxed affair.

I was looking out of the top window at the piece of blue sky and fluffy white cloud that I could see. As we were singing, in that same moment I thought, 'I'm going to miss you Pam,' not actually expecting a reply when suddenly, I heard her talking to me, telepathically you understand. Her words were these. 'Heather I'm not up there, I'm over here!' Immediately I looked over toward her coffin, and there she was, just as she said, as large as life, and as clear as daylight. My mouth dropped. I stopped singing. There was my friend, smiling at me, full of love and understanding, but also mischievous; after all she could see the look on my face! I wasn't afraid, just surprised, rather stunned, I wasn't expecting to see her. As I continued to just stare, she smiled and I heard her say or think, if you like, because her lips didn't move she just smiled, 'Come on this is a nice song,' and she began to conduct, waving her hand to the beat of the music. I knew Pam was also trying to cheer me up to show me that this wasn't a time for sadness. She was still alive, and I'd be able to see her again. So I tried to start singing once again but only a broken squeak came out, and I began to cry, then I couldn't see Pam anymore. She was probably still there listening to the service, but I had moved on to a lower level of consciousness and I lost contact with her.

After the service I felt exhilarated. I was so happy! I'd seen my friend, I knew she was happy, she was moving on to her next stage of evolution. Of course I'd miss her physical presence and I couldn't keep ringing her up if I needed a question answered.

I knew she'd taught me everything I needed to know; at least from her. She'd given me so much that I was grateful and happy I couldn't grieve anymore. If I ever needed confirmation of what I believed about life after death, Pam had made sure I had it; her last lesson and gift to me. So now I'd like to share what else I know about life after death with you.

Leaving the Body

The trouble with dying is that you feel so alive and well. It can be a bit hard to realise or believe that you have really died. For someone like Pam who was very aware and in touch with the spirit world, this experience wouldn't unsettle her for long, if at all. It would be fair to say that for every individual the experience of dying is a little bit different. The most classic example would be of the person who is ill in bed. Doctors, nurses or family members are able to report that, just before Uncle Fred died, he said he could see a bright light in the corner of the room or ceiling. Or, that a person in white was standing in the room waiting (often a spiritual guide or a loved one who had gone before them). Apparently, my granddad said to my nan that he could see someone standing in the corner of the room. For the dying person, this light, or the person waiting in white becomes so compelling that the soul, the consciousness, projects out toward the light being and breaks free of the physical body.

Reports from those who have had a near death experience, often say that, they seemed to float up to the ceiling, and were able to look down at the body on the bed, with feelings ranging from disinterest, repugnance, curiosity, sadness and even gratitude for all that the body experience had given to them. Most of these people also report feeling light and free from pain, fears, worries or cares. After they have seen enough, the newly departed spirit is escorted toward the light or they may follow a voice, or feel an attraction toward the light.

One of the best ways of making the transition from the physical to the spiritual world is during sleep state. I'm sure this would be most favoured by most of us, if we had a choice. The spirit travels much the same way that it travels on any night during our physical lives. That is to say via astral travel. We all do this, only on the occasion of our death the etheric silver cord that keeps us attached to our physical bodies breaks, and we can no longer go back to our bodies. These are two examples of an easy transition.

But what happens if you die suddenly, say in an accident of some kind? The spirit jumps out of the body quickly. This can be very confusing; to find your spirit self standing next to your physical self, perhaps looking rather lifeless, but your spirit self feels fine, if not better than ever.

'What is happening?' There may be confusion, the inability to make those around you, hear you or see you. You can no longer touch solid objects effectively, even though the spirit you feel's perfectly solid. A rather bewildering and disconcerting experience, until you realise new rules apply, such as telepathy. Moving objects with the mind or moving yourself by thought processes, i.e. one minute you are by the roadside the next you are at your mum's house twenty miles away. How did you get there? Then you are back following your body in the ambulance. How does this happen? You *thought* about the need to get in touch with mum, you *thought* about the need to follow your body. It's as simple as that! Once you work that out you may start feeling a bit more in control.

Of course the light comes as it comes for all, but we cannot be forced to go with it. If a spirit chooses, it can stay in the etheric world. This state is known as earthbound. Mostly, spirit people only stay here for a short while, say until after the funeral or until they are sure that their loved ones will be all right. Or perhaps to just take a last look around, not realising that they will be able to do this still, even after going to the light and entering the spirit world proper, if, they so desire it. This is quite a common thing for spirit people to do, when they are new to the spirit world. They come back to visit loved ones and favourite places etcetera, for the first few months after their physical death. But after a while the frequency of the visits drops off as the spirit world becomes more like home again. If a spirit seems to be stuck or unwilling to move on, perhaps because of a personal vendetta or some unfinished business, then rescue work is called for (I will cover this subject later on). For now let's assume our spirit friend has chosen to go toward the light, what happens then?

The Tunnel of Love

Sooner or later the spirit person accepts the call toward the light, which gets bigger and brighter. Some people will literally go through the ceiling and be able to look at the world below them, becoming distant. It should be said at this point that this is their perspective only, as the spirit world isn't really up there somewhere; it is rather all around. However it is on a higher vibration. Perhaps this is why people feel as if they are going up. Eventually everything goes into darkness, like a deep tunnel. This tunnel is a place of warmth and love; it gives a deep sense of security. As our spirit person travels through this tunnel, they may travel at great speed while others may float gently, walk or fly. They may become aware of other spirit people also travelling in the tunnel.

To begin with this warmth and love may be all that our spirit person needs if travelling alone, and they may choose to stay here for a little while; there is no hurry. It should also be said that the tunnel is also perceived in many different ways, i.e. a railway tunnel, maybe a black-hole vortex, or a kaleidoscope of colour. The journey back to the spirit world is real, but your perception of it is an individual experience, coloured by your subconscious beliefs, expectations, imagination etcetera. In the distance is the light at the end of the tunnel, getting brighter and brighter, drawing our spirit person closer and closer. A brightness so bright that with physical eyes you would not be able to look. The reason for this is that the higher the level of consciousness that we are on, the lighter our auric energy fields become.

In the spirit world, physical matter no longer encumbers our energy fields, and because love is the highest level of consciousness, the more love we express the lighter our energy field becomes. Our spirit person is about to be hit, so to speak, by more love than can be imagined. Where our Mr and Mrs Average are going is by no means the highest levels of consciousness. Suffice it to say that levels of finer light and love exist on higher levels of consciousness. So now our spirit person comes face to face with love and light. There are no barriers like walls, fences, rivers etcetera, to prevent his/her entry, as maybe found in a Near Death Experience. This time it's the real thing; our spirit person is going home!

Into the Light

On entering the light each spirit person's experiences, once again, are a little different. This is because we are all affected to a certain degree, by beliefs, and what we can feel comfortable with; i.e. you may be expecting harps, wings and clouds, on a conscious level, but on a deeper level you know it's better than that, and there must be more and therefore you are ready to transcend your conscious expectations.

The truth that is revealed to you is as much as you can comfortably accept at that moment in time. Does this mean that my spirit world is not real if you see it differently to me? Of course not, believe me it's a very real place! I will explain why we see things differently in the chapter about levels of consciousness. For now generally speaking, most people will find upon entering the light a world of immense beauty, where quite often loved ones who have died before them have gathered to meet and greet them. Amongst the many friends gathered there, are friends that have been known to them before they arrived on earth, but never actually knew. Amongst these will be our spirit person's true spiritual guides (those who have invisibly worked hard to guide them throughout their earthly life).

It is also at this point that many spirit people open up to the Christ consciousness, and may have an experience of being met by one of the many masters who have attained Christ consciousness. The Lord Jesus is but one master, among many, who have achieved Christ consciousness, but the Lord Jesus is also the most familiar master to many, whether they were of Christian origin or not. His love extends equally to all, regardless of religious background. However other masters do indeed come forward to greet spirits into the spirit world. Because Christ consciousness is universal it is therefore multidimensional, making it possible for a person to make contact, not only with Christ consciousness, but with the minds of the masters, and in particular the master with whom they feel the most affinity. Therefore personal interaction can take place between master and newly-arrived spirit person. More unconditional love than you can ever imagine seems to wrap around you and through you, and all the questions you have ever wanted answered, can be answered faster than you can speak the words. In fact, you don't have to speak, just think what you want to ask and via thought transference, a sort of highly-developed form of telepathy, unhindered by the physical body, you are given your answers. Don't forget, without a physical body you are now pure consciousness and so are your new companions, or should I say old companions. In reality we've known each other since the beginning of time.

After our initial welcome home so to speak, our friends and loved ones will be around to help us get reacquainted with our new/old home; the spirit world. And, of course, getting used to using our minds to create things, go places, speak to each other, so on and so forth. Unlike the physical world, in the spirit world our thoughts have instant reactions, so you can see how this skill may take a bit of practice. But most spirit people are reacquainted with them quite quickly, as they also begin to discover the beauties of the wonderful spirit world. However although our spirit person can go off with his or her friends and loved ones on a sojourn of delights, one very important experience has to take place. There isn't a choice. Sooner or later we are all called upon to experience this. And so next our spirit person goes with the spiritual guides that were always with him or her throughout the physical life to experience the life review.

The Life Review

People tend to think of this as something to be feared; Judgement Day! The moment when we are either admitted to Heaven or condemned to hell. The truth is that this image couldn't be further from the truth. With the help of our spiritual guides we are shown what could be described as a video recording of our life on earth. The video recording is in fact our own consciousness, and that of others we have mixed with during our lifetime, either directly or indirectly. Gathered together and focused in front of us, so that we can view it. We interpret this as being a kind of tape being played back.

Our spiritual guides are not there to judge us, but to lend loving support as we are guided through the life review experience. The purpose of the life review isn't to judge us. It is to show us how the choices, decisions, actions and reactions that we take during our lifetime have affected our spiritual growth and how we have affected all others that we came into contact with in our lifetime. We are shown our good deeds and our not-so-good deeds, and the ripple effects and consequences these have. As we go through the life review we are able to experience the feelings that others have experienced as a result of our actions; even thoughts we have behind someone's back have a knock on effect. At any time the video so to speak, can be stopped, so that we can discuss any points in greater detail. The idea of the life review isn't to punish us or to make us squirm. It's to help us see with spiritual eyes what we failed to see on earth. It also shows us our achievements and contributions to man's evolutionary progress. In this way we can judge ourselves, not as we judge on earth, but from a spiritual point of view. With the help of our spiritual guides, we can see what progress we have made and where we have fallen down. Also where our souls still need to make improvement.

Once we are agreed on what we need still to learn and correct etcetera, we are free to enjoy the spirit world and relax, until our souls are called to work out a plan for their return to earth. This is better known as reincarnation; I will go into this subject in more detail later on. In the meantime there is much to enjoy and experience in the spirit world, much to learn, and if we so desire many things that we can do of a helpful nature, e.g. healing work. For example, even spirit people need healing from emotional and mental trauma. Also healing people on earth, by coming through a physical spiritual healer. Then there is rescue work. That is helping those who have physically died, and are not yet aware of it, or are having difficulty accepting it.

Teaching skills can be put to good use, sharing experience with souls who may need a similar experience, looking after children or animals; there are so many worthwhile jobs that you can train for. You could sit on a cloud strumming a harp if you really want to, but I bet you'll find something better to do! Some of the skills we have learned here on earth can be continued in the spirit world: writing music, for instance, architecture, (designed and built with the mind) gardening, painting, to name but a few. The big difference is of course that everything is done by thought form. We create with our minds. If you want to create, for instance, the building of a matchstick boat with your hands, for the sheer pleasure of it, you can. You have only to desire it. If you want to create a house full of dust to clean up till it's spick and span, you can create dust from your thoughts, your memories, but dust itself doesn't exist in the spirit world as such. Dust is physical.

There are wonderful halls of learning, halls of history, art, music, libraries – my husband's particular favourite as a lover of books! We joke about him putting his name down to work in libraries! To try and describe the wonders of the spirit world would take volumes. The music, the colours, the exquisite flowers, the trees and grass, no weeds! Buildings like translucent marble, everything beautiful and perfectly formed. So much which I'd like to share with you but I'd be sidetracking from the point of this book, so, instead, I will list some recommended reading at the back. So what happens if you get stuck for some reason, and you can't or won't move toward the light? What if you find yourself in a living hell? It happens, but God doesn't send you to hell. If you find yourself there it's because you put yourself there! Who in their right mind would do such a thing? 'Right mind' are the key words! In the next chapter I hope things will become clearer.

Chapter Two
IN MY FATHER'S HOUSE THERE ARE MANY MANSIONS

WHEN I WAS A LITTLE GIRL, AND I FIRST HEARD THE WORDS, 'In my Father's house there are many mansions,' I thought that was what it meant literally, that in Heaven there are many mansions – big fancy buildings. After all, if Jesus said it, then it must be true. What I didn't realise then, was that Jesus often used symbolic language in order to get a point across. Now I am older and have had time to reflect on the Lord's words, I understand what he meant much better. It may well be true that there are many mansion-type buildings in the spirit world, since our thoughts can create just about anything we desire, but that isn't quite what the Lord was referring to. What I do believe he was referring to are the many planes of existence that make up the spirit world we know as Heaven, or as Jesus referred to them as his father's house. So what are these planes of existence? I firmly believe the planes of existence to be levels of consciousness, of which there are many.

These planes of existence exist within much broader planes. These planes are known as the *etheric*, the *emotional* or *astral*, the *mental* plane, and beyond these the *heavenly* planes. I cannot tell you anything about the heavenly planes, and my knowledge of the mental planes at this instant is not enough to write with any confidence. However I can explain the etheric plane and the emotional thought planes, better known as the astral planes, or, more precisely, the upper and lower astral planes. I'd like to start with the upper astral plane. First as it is not only the more pleasant, but also the plane that most people will gravitate to naturally after death. The astral planes are also where we go to during sleep, and the dream state. When we astral travel, and we all do whether we are consciously aware of it or not, it is to the astral planes that we go. Also known as the emotional realm, the realms of desire, the place where we can create anything we desire. The place we can paint like a great artist, sing like an angel. We can fly, sink a pint in our favourite pub, or clean a house full of dust if that's what we really want to do. Actually the astral planes are much more than this. We go there to meet friends, some living, and some dead. It's where we go to meet our spiritual guides, when we seek guidance for our everyday problems. It's where we go to rest when we die. It's a place of learning, of spiritual growth; a place of fun and happiness. It offers opportunities to help others, to heal and to teach.

In order to really explain you need to understand who you are more fully, for you are not just the physical body that you see in the mirror each morning. You are spirit, or pure consciousness. When your spirit leaves your physical body you are no longer confined. Your consciousness seems to expand. Your consciousness consists of all of your memories, your thoughts, feelings, experiences, and your subconscious memories, including those from before you came to earth. Your spiritual mission is also held here. Everything that is you, all that your soul has experienced, past lives, how we came to be, everything, absolutely everything! The more you experience the more your consciousness expands, the higher becomes your conscious mind. The more it expands the more information opens up for you to access. Likewise the lower your conscious mind, the smaller it gets, the less information is open to you, i.e. open-minded expands, small-minded closes in on itself. This is important to understand, as you will see as we explore the upper and lower astral planes.

The astral planes are a real place, made of the same energy as planet earth, but because the energy vibrates at a faster rate it would not seem solid or fixed, but more fluid and flexible from our point of view. When you are there you are also vibrating at a faster rate; therefore the astral plane that you reside on seems every bit as solid to you as earth did. The difference is in the way that everything is created, with the mind and emotions. The energy that creates a pretty little cottage with roses around the door is your energy. Your desire to see it, to have it, brings it into being. But if you have a belief that you are not quite worthy of such a wonderful gift, your subconscious mind battling with your conscious mind, then the cottage you are trying to create will fade in and out of consciousness and will not become fixed. However once you fix your sights on something properly, it materialises properly and becomes fixed, at least for as long as you want it to. If you should tire of the cottage, it will gradually disintegrate. As you think less about it, you begin to withdraw your energy from it until eventually it no longer exists. The energy it took to form your creation becomes pure energy again and can be reused. But should you discover a while down the lane, so to speak, that you miss the cottage, and you'd like it back, well no problem, the memory of it is within you; just think it back into existence. You don't even have to plan out all the details this time around. Incidentally, there are plenty of people there who will help you with architecture, design and construction, if building and DIY is not your forte. Our creations only last as long as we are interested in them. As we evolve and change, so do our desires and creations.

Can Anyone Else See Your Cottage?

Because like attracts like, you will find that like-minded spirit people are attracted to the same level of consciousness as you. As your consciousness blends with another consciousness perhaps a friend, aunt or brother; whoever – you share automatically your experiences, although it's possible to know everything there is to know about the companion you have blended with. You give your attention to what they are focusing on at the time. This may sound complicated, but it isn't really. You don't have to think about it. You do it automatically. Blending consciousness isn't unique to the spirit world. We do it all the time on earth. As you sit with a friend you are blending your energies, but the physical body's density acts like a filter, so we are not aware of every thought our companions have. In the spirit world there are no such barriers. So the spirit person quickly learns to focus on one thing at a time, and can ignore the rest. In this way privacy is honoured. On earth those with clairvoyant ability learn how to switch off from what they can see in another's energy field. It's the same in the spirit world.

So can anyone else see your cottage? Of course they can, although the cottage is made of your mind energy, it does not stay within your mind. Your desire to have the cottage means that you project your energy out onto the fixed landscape, and there you leave it. At least for as long as you desire it. Therefore not only can you draw their attention to it, show them around etcetera, but also because it is part of the fixed landscape, everyone on that level of consciousness can see it. It has become part of the fixed landscape. Not everyone will notice it if they are preoccupied. Talking of landscape, what a beautiful landscape it is. Rolling hills and planes, crystal clear rivers and streams of living water, flowers of such beauty and colours, unlike the colours we have here, each plant emitting its own vibratory note. You will only hear them if you want to. You are surrounded by constant music, in a way, but you are not constantly focused on it, even though it is so beautiful and so totally harmonious. There are halls of learning, healing etcetera which, along with the landscape, are constantly fixed and have been created for us by God and higher evolved souls. A perfect paradise to which we can add our own creations. A place not unlike earth, yet far superior. Created so that we may have familiarity and feel comfortable when we arrive there. Perhaps these planes of existence are what the Bible refers to as the Garden of Eden. The place where we existed before man's descent to earth.

What if someone you have loved on earth now resides on a different level of consciousness to you, can you meet with him or her again? Yes you can, if you are on a higher level of consciousness it will be up to you to meet on their level or a mutually comfortable level, because as the vibrational rate becomes faster, it's a bit like climbing a mountain; the air gets thinner so to speak. A faster rate would be uncomfortable to someone who is used to a slower rate; it is always easier to lower your rate. But to rise up to a level you have never experienced, even temporarily, requires help, until you evolve naturally. So what happens? You want to meet Uncle Fred who's on a lower level than you. Well you don't have to think, 'I'll have to lower my consciousness, slow down my vibrations,' all you do is think of Uncle Fred, desire to be with him, and you will be there. What if Uncle Fred wants to see you? As he thinks of you, you pick up his telepathic message and you can go to him. If you are busy doing something all-absorbing, you can send a telepathic message, or a messenger. How about being in both places at once? After all, we are multidimensional souls, but that may take a bit of learning. So, for now, let's get back to Uncle Fred. You can be with him in an instant or, if you prefer, you can walk, drive a car, anything you want to. I should say, at this point, that there is no traffic, as such, in the spirit world, except, for any personal vehicle you may like to temporarily create for the sheer pleasure of the experience. If Uncle Fred is not where you expected him to be when you arrive, another thought will put you in touch with his location. Or if you prefer, you can always ask someone!

The Changing Scenery

As your thoughts change and your vibrations move either faster or slower, so the scenery before you will become fluid again and the scene before your eyes will start to melt away, and a new scene will take shape. As you go higher the scene becomes finer and more beautiful. You would not feel comfortable there for very long unless you had evolved to that level. To reach higher without having evolved you would need to rise on the energy of another, more advanced soul. To go lower is easier, but you would still not find it comfortable for long periods. It would be denser and less beautiful, less bright, but it would not necessarily be unpleasant to go lower, unless you were thinking of going very much lower. If you wanted to do some rescue work, you would have to be a very advanced soul who could cope, and would be aware. If you were not, it could be a threatening experience as it is easy to get immersed in the more negative energy that makes up these planes of existence.

Hell

The lower levels of the astral plane, traditionally known as the place of hellfire and brimstone! Starring a devil in a red suit with horns, a tail and a pitchfork with which to prod you. I cannot say for certain that such a place doesn't exist, but what I can say is that hell is your own creation. There are as many hells as your imagination is able to create. Therefore the archetypal image of hell could be created, if you believe in it enough, and worse, if you believe at some level of consciousness that you deserve it. In other words hell exists for you because, at a deeper level, you let it!

These levels of consciousness are dark and dingy because people's minds are closed with negative thought. A closed mind withdraws into itself. They literally live within their own minds, rather than blending with others around them. They are very often alone, within themselves, and therefore within a world of their own creation. They cannot see anyone else there, even though there are plenty of others sharing the same plane of existence. They only share the company of people of their own creative minds. The mind is so powerful as to be able to create some pretty convincing horrors.

So are all the people who find themselves on this level of consciousness wicked people? No, of course not. Surprisingly, many are fairly average people. Perhaps they made a mistake or two, it played on their mind, they felt guilt-ridden, unable to forgive themselves. Perhaps they are bitter about something, depressed or a suicide victim. The thoughts of their past deeds are so overpowering and all-consuming, even if they have been relegated to the subconscious mind during life.

Once out of the physical body the consciousness expands and amplifies. The most powerful thoughts become dominant. The soul continues then to play out the scenarios again and again. That in itself is torture. Others will add to this a need for punishment and create, albeit unconsciously, an appropriate punishment. Perhaps they may play out a court scene and go through being condemned by a jury sentenced by a judge and executed over and over again. For others they may just feel and experience despair, sinking into darker darkness and heavy depression. The ability to create is infinite, only restricted by our lack of imagination; spirit people do not realise that they are living within the confines of their own minds at this level. The horrors that surround them are all their own creations.

Rescue Work

These people do not have to stay in this lower level of existence. It is not a case of once you have found your level that is where you must stay. It is a self-imposed prison. They usually do not realise this. Perhaps they cannot forgive themselves or maybe they harbour feelings of bitterness and resentment toward another person that they knew whilst on earth. But whatever keeps them there, they can be stuck for a very long time, even centuries of earth time. They have no concept of time. Just by raising their consciousness to a higher level they could find themselves in a happier realm where healing, help and advice can be given, and a way to deal with the torment or unfinished business can be found. These people are not aware of this until perhaps they call to God for help. As soon as they do that they have raised their consciousness and have expanded their minds enough to see the light in the distance, and someone will be able to come forward to help them.

These helpers are known as rescue workers. Although many souls both living on earth and living in spirit carry out rescue work, it is only very advanced souls who venture down to the lower astral planes because of the negative energy, and the danger of becoming engulfed by it. These souls are not only waiting for the cry for help, before they go in to attempt a rescue. They are also constantly trying to get through to these people. They try to penetrate the consciousness of the tormented souls, but this is not easy as it is a bit like getting through to someone in a coma. Even the advanced soul can stay only a short while at a time. If and when they are successful, they can then take the tormented souls to their natural level of consciousness. However no soul can ever be forced to go toward the light.

At even lower levels are the souls stuck in a consciousness of depraved sexual practices, devil worship, black magic, the sadistic and masochistic minds.

Psychologists would have a field day if they could go there and see for themselves. They would be literally looking into other people's minds. It can be an utterly sick and frightening experience. It would be very dangerous, as you yourself could become stuck there by your own fears and hang-ups. Being in a negative consciousness will amplify and bring to the forefront your own negativity.

Even lower is the elemental spirit realm. These elemental spirits are a blend of negative energy and come from the pool of collective consciousness, created by our fears and beliefs and negative thoughts and actions toward each other. Someone on earth going through a bad nightmare or experiencing a 'bad trip', whilst using drugs, will often experience this level of consciousness.

These elementals take on the forms of creatures, monsters, devils etcetera that exist in the collective consciousness. They are our thought forms, and elemental spirits feed on our strongest thought forms and archetypal images. Since like attracts like, you automatically attract to yourself the things that you fear most of all.

Hell, I feel, will only exist as long as mankind continues to create his or her own hell. In other words, when we start treating each other and ourselves with kindness and respect etcetera, we will automatically raise our consciousness to the higher levels. The lower levels will eventually become redundant, the energy left there i.e. negative thought forms will eventually dissipate as we stop thinking negatively. Stop feeding the fire so to speak! The energy will be freed up again to be used hopefully in a positive way instead.

Let's leave the lower astral planes now, and take a sojourn back into the higher astral planes. By raising our consciousness on to higher and better things, watch as the darker realms start to melt away before your very eyes! Like magic the scenery before you becomes, once again better, more beautiful and lighter. The atmosphere is much finer, not so heavy or oppressive. The dirty negative pollution gives way to a crystal clear atmosphere.

That's the wonderful thing about the higher realms, it's impossible to feel miserable there, and once you have made it to the higher realms your worries, fears and problems are over; at least for now. Any healing that needs to take place on earth will take place in good time through reincarnation, but for now it's time to relax.

So what about the religious side of the astral planes? Well all religions exist in the astral planes, because some people desire to continue to practice their chosen religion as they did on earth. And, of course, you can join a religious group if you feel an affinity with one, even if you didn't belong on earth. I suspect that similar rules apply to membership requirements. Spirit people are free to gather together whenever they are with like-minded people.

Many souls recognise that religion can be a catalyst to help you get back to God. It is an opportunity to learn such things as faith, trust and discipline but it is not the only way toward evolving spiritually nor even the end of the soul's journey. However a sojourn within a particular religion can be a welcome and needed experience for the soul whilst on earth, as it will provide wonderful opportunities for spiritual growth. Therefore it is natural that some personalities should want to continue, for a while at least, with their chosen religious practice whilst on the astral planes. As the soul evolves and grows, the need for organised religion becomes less, as the soul expands beyond the restrictions of organised religions. Having said this, belonging to a religion can offer a soul-expanding experience, in its own right, for the riches that such an experience can give. Therefore, just as religion should not be forced upon a person, neither should a person be discouraged from their choice. (Dangerous cult groups are a different matter.)

In time, and not before all souls are completely ready, religions will pass away, as souls become more in tune with Christ consciousness. There will be no need to stay with the catalyst that tries to encourage us closer to the Christ consciousness that is within each and everyone of us. From time to time we reach it during our lifetime if we are lucky. One day we will all be living it constantly as we eventually master it ourselves.

Another question that is often raised concerning the spirit world is sex. People often ask me this one, albeit sheepishly. Do we or don't we? Happily I can say yes we do! We don't stop just because we don't have a physical body. We still desire to love and to express that love. Some sources indicate that sex is a much more satisfying experience as you merge and blend more completely with your beloved. Since your thoughts and feelings are amplified in the spirit world, we can only imagine how wonderful an experience it will be! And on that vibrational note perhaps it might be a good moment to make our move down to the etheric plane.

The Etheric Level

The etheric plane of existence is the one closest to the earth plane, and surrounds the earth. It is the earth's spiritual counterpart. Everything on earth has an etheric double. Whether it is animate or inanimate, animal, vegetable, mineral, everything is created from God's energy. It's just that on the physical plane the energy moves at a slower rate and therefore everything appears to be solid. The etheric counterpart is an exact copy of the physical; or to be precise the physical is an exact copy of the etheric. Everything begins life with a thought. The physical is the thought made manifest. You design a table first in your mind. Perhaps you reject the first idea because the legs are wrong, so you redesign the table that you will eventually make. Now the paper you drew it on has an etheric counterpart in the etheric plane. The same happens with the finished table; both the drawing and the finished table have a permanent etheric counterpart, or at least until you destroy the table. Then its etheric counterpart will also disintegrate slowly. How about the original design, the one with the legs that were wrong? Well that too would have started to form an etheric counterpart in the ether, but as soon as you dropped the idea it would begin to fade, and would disappear much quicker because you didn't think about it enough for the etheric counterpart to form properly. Whatever we form in thought strongly and regularly enough will eventually manifest in physical form. Now you can begin to see how useful or dangerous our thoughts can be. But I digress.

You may have heard how someone who has a leg or arm amputated says they can still feel it days or weeks after the leg has gone. What they can feel is the etheric energy counterpart, until it dissipates. Perhaps if we could hang on to the idea that we still have a leg instead of accepting that we have lost it completely, it could regrow. After all the DNA still exists. What a fascinating and, some might say, crazy far-fetched idea, but is it? We create with our minds every day; it's really just a matter of how much you can believe. You can move mountains – they are only piles of molecules etcetera! When we die, or should I say, leave our physical body permanently, our etheric double will eventually disintegrate. However your appearance remains in your memory bank and therefore your image can be recreated at will. However most people prefer the younger more perfect version of themselves, which automatically transpires as they spend more time in the higher astral planes.

In Chapter One we looked at what happens immediately after a spirit leaves the physical body.

It is the etheric level that spirit people, who have just died, tend to stay on for a while. Perhaps because they haven't understood that they have died, or perhaps they want to make sure that their loved ones are going to be all right. Maybe they love their home so much, or are concerned about their work. Maybe they want to get even with someone. Whatever the reason for staying, or however long they stay on the etheric plane, they are in a state known as earthbound. Eventually a spirit person will move on. However they can still return to the etheric plane to visit loved ones or their favourite pub if they want to. But by now the etheric body has disintegrated, although the astral body is still recognisable as our dearly departed, whether the image that is projected is the old lady or the younger rejuvenated lady. A spirit person may draw close to the etheric plane to give a message to a medium, to be close to a loved one, say, on an anniversary, or to comfort someone who is suffering prolonged grieving. Many people do not realise that to grieve excessively can actually keep a loved one's spirit earthbound, and therefore hinder their spiritual progress, not to mention make them unhappy as they worry about the loved one back on earth.

Our loved ones are but a thought away. However it does require the slowing down of their vibrations in order to come to us here on the earth plane, and it can be hard work.

Let us have a look at a newly departed spirit who finds itself in the etheric plane. Let's assume that he's found his feet a bit, and he decides to visit his favourite pub. He can be there just by thinking of it; he can go through the door if he wants. But walls won't be a problem either as he can go right through. Now what about that pint of bitter? Well his favourite barmaid may be on tonight but unless she has the ability she cannot see him, couldn't serve him anyway, he cannot hold the glass, so what can he do? He can create an etheric pint of bitter. He can even create his own barmaid to serve him. She can have all the curves in all the right places, make perfect conversation, he can even touch her as she will feel like flesh and blood to him, but she won't have a soul. Anyway he has his pint; it tastes as good as the best pint he can remember. But if he's never had a pint of bitter before then it will taste of whatever he imagines it to taste of. Sometimes it will taste of nothing at all. Now to his favourite chair, the one by the fireplace. Oh no! Someone's in his seat. He tries asking the person to move. They don't hear. But if he is lucky and the person is receptive enough he can try telepathy that might work. Your unsuspecting earth person may suddenly decide to change to another table, but if they don't, what then? Adopt plan B and create your own seat near the fire. If our spirit person is a stubborn sort he may try sitting on the earth person. This gives a strange sensation to the earth person who may feel shivers, or tingling etcetera as the two energies, with different vibrational rates, blend together.

In time, the spirit person becomes bored, or disenchanted with this level of existence. Even though he may have met other spirit people that he can share his time with, the beckoning call deep inside tells him there is better than this and it's time to move on. Our spirit person naturally gravitates toward the level of consciousness that he will feel most comfortable on.

Chapter Three

SUICIDE

I T STILL SADDENS ME, AND TO SOME EXTENT FRIGHTENS ME, having learnt as a child that some religions hold the belief that suicide is an unpardonable sin against God, and the gift of life, and if you commit suicide you could not be buried in consecrated ground. Therefore your soul would not be able to enter Heaven. That by your own doing you would condemn yourself to eternal torment. That kind of belief system is enough to frighten anyone let alone a young impressionable adolescent. Fortunately for me I question things a lot. I couldn't believe that God, who I had been assured is a God of Love, would be without compassion for someone who is in a state of despair, deep enough to take their own life. This wasn't right. Somehow, there must be a flaw somewhere. After all if I could feel pity for someone who commits suicide, then surely God who is pure love would have even more compassion and a better understanding than me. So I wasn't buying that scenario of God turning his back on a suicide victim, and sending them to a life of eternal torment! Love is never cruel. I didn't know what the answer was at the time but I felt pretty sure that eternal torment wasn't part of God's divine plan. Despite such damaging teachings I respectfully questioned this God I was taught to fear, love and see as my father in Heaven. I·thought, if God is my father, he won't mind if I question him. After all, it says in the Bible, 'If any of you lack wisdom let him ask of God,' so I did.

In fact over the years I have talked to God so much, I think he has probably bought an answer machine to take my calls!

Seriously though, I have received answers to my prayers and as a result have been able to formulate a new understanding of God and his divine plan. I'm happy to say that this includes a God who is truly all love, compassion and great understanding. In God's Heaven, is the offer to all souls of the opportunity to put right the wrongs and continue with their spiritual development.

So, back to suicide, what really happens to a person who commits suicide? Well in theory after death this soul would travel toward the light just as anyone else, be embraced by the light and love, meet loved ones and spiritual guides just as anyone else. From there they may be taken to a place of healing, should they need it, where they can rest and recover a while. Their death and reasons for committing suicide, in the first place, were more than likely very traumatic and painful. Although they no longer have a physical body, the mental and emotional side to them still needs healing. In time, when a soul is fit enough, a life review is experienced; this usually is quite quickly after arrival in the spirit world. Everybody goes through this, not just suicide victims, usually accompanied by our spiritual guides, who try to help us on our journey, as examined in Chapter One. We can judge our actions and reactions ourselves to see what improvements we need to make. God does not judge us. This done, all souls have the opportunity to rest in the spirit world and enjoy all that it has to offer, until it is time for our soul to make another journey into the physical world.

Before we move on I should point out that our spiritual guides are there to guide us and help us, not to live our lives for us. They cannot force us to listen to our intuition; neither can they stop us from committing suicide, because they cannot interfere with our free will.

This, then, is a brief description of what should happen when someone commits suicide. However what usually happens is quite different and very sad.

As I explained in the last chapter, the spirit world is a world of pure consciousness. We are pure consciousness, restrained to a certain degree by our physical body. When we die, we become pure consciousness unrestrained. As I've said before, the spirit world is made up of levels of consciousness, generally known as the astral planes. When we leave our physical bodies, whether permanently when we die, or as we do regularly during sleep and dream state, we naturally gravitate towards a level of consciousness that we feel comfortable with, but also a level that reflects our state of mind at the time, i.e. the more loving, happy and selfless our thoughts and feelings are, the higher the level of consciousness we will gravitate towards. This area is known as the upper astral planes. Likewise the lower astral planes are the lower levels of consciousness, where we express thoughts that are negative, self-pitying, depressing etcetera.

Therefore it is to the lower astral planes that many suicide victims will find themselves gravitating to naturally, because of their unhappy state of mind at the time of death, along also with feelings of guilt and self-imposed unworthiness about their right to go to 'heaven'. As in all levels of consciousness, because our bodies no longer restrict us, thoughts and feelings become amplified. We no longer live so much with our minds, we are our minds! Every soul's thoughts and feelings help to create the atmosphere of the level of consciousness that they occupy. Love, happiness and beauty, as associated with Heaven, or misery, depression and ugliness, as is associated with hell. And so suicide victims find themselves in a world where their thoughts, feelings and ideas about their problems are projected all around them. No longer restricted in their heads, except now they no longer have a body, and therefore do not have the means to sort out the problem.

Some of these souls will keep reliving past events that lead up to their suicide. At this stage it is unlikely that they are aware that they are creating this self-imposed scenario of misery and suffering themselves. (A bit like acting out a play over and over again.) They don't realise that by changing their thoughts to self-love, forgiveness and compassion they can find themselves quickly moving toward the light.

At some stage they will realise that suicide was a very big mistake, which unfortunately adds to their misery, because it didn't solve the problems they tried to escape from. In fact, in the spirit world, our problems are amplified. Our suicide victim starts to realise how precious life is, and that it is the only way to solve the problems that we experience on earth. On top of this, if you believe that suicide is an unforgivable sin; that God will turn his back on you, that you will be condemned to eternal hell for what you have done, then the chances are that you will believe that this place that you find yourself in is God's punishment, and just what you deserve. As you can see, it isn't that difficult to add to the state of depression, but it is much harder to get out of. No wonder it is likened to hell! As I've said before, God doesn't punish us, we constantly punish ourselves when we allow ourselves to live in a state of negativity all of the time, believing that our problems have no solution.

This self-imposed state of hell can cause victims to be trapped for many years, centuries even. So does nobody care? Of course they do. Souls who are more spiritually aware will try to reach the suicide victims and persuade them to think differently. They try to explain the truth of the situation in the hope that they may see the light. But at the end of the day it's up to the suicide victim; nobody can do it for them, nor can they be forced to abandon their misery. The souls who try to help the suicide victim are known as rescue workers, as I have described in the last chapter. The task of these gallant souls is both difficult and dangerous. Although they never give up, it can take a long time!

However, once help is accepted, our victim very quickly finds themselves moving up to the higher levels of consciousness where healing can take place.

The Lord Jesus taught that 'as a man thinketh so shall he become', and also, 'as you believe be it unto you'. I believe the Lord was trying to teach us that our thoughts, feelings and beliefs are the tools that create our reality, our experience.

Some suicide victims realise that they need their physical body in order to overcome their problems and complete the work they were meant to complete whilst on earth. They are not necessarily aware of our soul's ability to reincarnate, and so out of desperation they attempt to use the body of a living person. Perhaps they will try to use the body of a family member, and try to get them to do their will. This is a futile attempt, as the living person has their own path to lead, and must live their own life. Nobody else can live your life or learn your lessons for you. However, in the attempt, a suicide victim can wreak havoc, and cause a lot of problems to the person whom they have chosen to try to work through; as this true story will demonstrate.

★

Dawn very kindly gave her permission for me to give her real name.

Dawn came to see me for reflexology because she had suffered with very severe headaches for many years, and yet medical tests showed time and again that their was nothing wrong with her, at least not physically, and it was suggested that perhaps there was a psychological problem.

Dawn was naturally very upset, and admitted to me that she did wonder if she might have a problem, but wanted to try reflexology first as it was recommended as being highly effective as a treatment against migraines; which it is.

However after several weeks of treatment and some improvement, it didn't seem to be effective enough. Quite by chance or perhaps not by chance at all, Dawn started to ask me about my NFSH certificate on the wall, and wanted to learn about spiritual healing. So I began talking a bit about healing, what I do and what sort of experiences I had. It was then that Dawn really began to open up and explain her headache problems more clearly.

Up until then she had only told me about her stressful lifestyle and everyday things. Now, suddenly, Dawn started to explain how she didn't feel as if her mind was her own at times; that she didn't feel in control of her thoughts. She became naturally upset, as she expressed her thoughts, that she might be going crazy. She also told me that she always felt cold down her left side.

At this point a bell started to ring within me. I wondered if some earthbound spirit might have attached itself to her in some way. I asked Dawn if she could try to remember when her headaches had started. To my surprise she could remember quite clearly. They had started quite soon after her father had committed suicide, and soon after she moved house. Once the headaches began, they very soon got worse. Before long Dawn was having a headache everyday. In fact Dawn began to accept the fact that she would start each day with painkillers. She explained that if she didn't take one before the headache got going, as she put it, she'd have a blinder all day and, as it was, she always had a dull ache.

I realise that we can create pain and illness in our bodies, with our thoughts and affirmations. Such statements as, 'I always wake up with a headache every morning,' will encourage the subconscious mind to oblige. But this was much more than this. I realised that there was a pretty good chance that her father had attached himself to his daughter. I also knew that no amount of reflexology, conventional medicine, psychiatrists, etcetera would be of any help at all. This would require spiritual help, healing and rescue work. I've done a lot of what I call distant cleansing and clearing work, but I had never worked directly with the client. It's the same process, but it was a first for me, and took a bit more courage on my part. Therefore I told Dawn the truth; 'I know what to do but this is a first for me.' I needn't have worried. Dawn trusted me and wanted me to go ahead. I felt I'd be happier if my husband could stand in with us. Dawn didn't mind. He very kindly obliged but said he didn't know what use he could be. He was my moral support and that was good enough for me!

With everyone assembled, I began with a prayer for protection, guidance and assistance. As I began I could see in my mind's eye, the descending shaft of light, and also a silhouette of a man who seemed to be half-in and half-out of her body – (no wonder she felt so cold down one side all of the time). He appeared to have very curly hair but I could not see his face as he was all black. However I could feel deep depression and despair. He felt so heavy; it was as if he were made of lead. The feeling would have been overwhelming except that I felt detached from the situation, rather than a part of it. I felt only compassion and love for this man and his desperate and futile attempt to complete his life mission through his daughter's body. Over time his depression would have mounted as his frustration grew. With my mind I started to speak to him. I tried to explain that he should go toward the light that was waiting for him, and let Dawn lead her own life, but he wouldn't budge. So I tried again, kindly but firmly explaining that, in the light, he would find help and healing; that he really must let go and let Dawn get on as he was hindering her progress. But, no way! He clung on for dear life; he wasn't going anywhere. Telepathy is quite hard work. Anyway I tried again, I told him that if he went toward the light he would get help to prepare for a new body, so that he could finish whatever was needed. This seemed to do the trick. I saw the man pull himself free from Dawn's side and walk, albeit very slowly, toward the light. His feet seemed leaden like the boots divers used to wear. As he reached the beam of light that was waiting for him it was as if a floor started to raise him up within the light, like a lift. About halfway up the man tried to get out. I sensed a feeling that he didn't feel worthy to go any higher. Quite firmly I told him to wait and carry on up. I could see hands reaching down to him. I told him, 'They are waiting for you.' With that he gave himself into their care. Before he went, he turned, blew his daughter a kiss, and went with the light as it ascended out of my sight. In my heart I knew that this man was Dawn's father. I finished with a prayer and thanked Heaven for their help. I knew that he would be all right from now on, and so, too, I felt, would Dawn. After I brought Dawn around, I told her what had taken place and what I had seen. Dawn told me that her dad had had a mop of curly black hair. For all I knew he could have been completely bald. This was all the proof that I needed Dawn's father was on his way to being healed at last. Dawn would need some more healing, (which we began there and then) as I felt that her own auric energy field would have a large hole, and that some healing and sealing would be necessary, as she might be vulnerable to other people's negative energy, illness etcetera. Straight away Dawn was aware that the cold feeling had left her.

I next saw Dawn after the Christmas holiday. She reported that the headaches were considerably better and not so frequent, but not yet completely gone. I reminded her that she had lived with headaches for so long that her mind was programmed to expect a headache. I felt sure that in time things would improve naturally, but if they didn't hypnotherapy would help to get rid of the suggestion that a headache was inevitable.

The last time I saw Dawn, not only was she well, but her whole life had changed for the better as well as the lives of her family. This, then, is a successful and happy end to our story, but it does make me wonder how many other desperate souls are out there, and how many so called psychological cases are in fact something similar to this one!

Of course, suicide is not the answer. Life is a precious gift, designed to help us grow spiritually. Suicide cannot be condoned, but neither should it be judged. To judge is not our privilege. God has a divine plan that includes the opportunity for us to put right our mistakes, whatever they may be. God does not judge, God is pure Love. Judgement is an earthly concept not a spiritual one. Once a suicide victim reaches the light they very soon realise the mistake he or she has made. The work they did not complete successfully, the spiritual mission unfulfilled, the inevitable delay to their spiritual evolution, the pain they have caused to loved ones and the completion of work needed to be carried out with loved ones, now delayed. They know how foolish suicide is. Any suffering is borne out of that knowledge and any punishment is irrelevant.

Chapter Four
WHO AND WHAT IS GOD?

I T WOULD BE VERY DANGEROUS FOR ME TO SUGGEST TO YOU that I know all the answers to this question. I am quite sure that in reality, I know very little, but what I can say is that my understanding of who and what God is, has grown somewhat since my early Sunday school days.

Most of us have been introduced at sometime or another to the image of a kindly elderly gentleman, with a long grey beard and flowing white robes; with a thunder bolt in one hand and a little lamb tucked under his other arm; sandal clad feet and a choir of heavenly angels and cherubs with halos and wings and trumpets.

This glorious image is also accompanied by God's somewhat dubious and very human characteristics. He, (note He) is a God of love and purity, who blesses the meek and mild, the humble in spirit, the lowly and self-sacrificing etcetera. However, he is also a very angry and jealous God, who brings down his wrath (the thunder bolt) on the sinful and wicked, who metes out blessings and miracles to some, and ignores the prayers of others. Giving health and happiness to some, and misery and suffering to others. That's just whilst we are on earth! When we are in Heaven, (let's assume we arrive before Saint Peter, God's faithful servant with the big book marked, 'This is your Life') all the good bits and bad bits are ticked off and weighed up then judged. We stand before God, knees trembling and fingers crossed. But an all seeing God announces, 'That won't do any good. I can see you crossing your fingers behind your back.' I exaggerate, but you get the picture!

Nearly every religion I have come across seems to believe that being a member of their church will stand you in good stead, as they are, 'God's chosen, and favoured', and as such, the members can expect to ascend to the top; the best part of Heaven, (subject to leading a good life according to the religion's standards). But the rest of us must make do with a lower Heaven. I don't mean to sound unkind, but such a teaching does sound rather narrow and arrogant.

There are some pretty saintly people out there, who do a lot of good. Will God really say, 'Sorry you're not in the chosen religion, so I'm afraid you'll have to make do with my lesser Heaven?'

Then of course if you are not worthy of Heaven, woe betides you. It's hellfire and brimstone for you. Eternal torment and a lot of prodding by a red devil with horns, tail and a pitchfork.

It's hard to believe that for hundreds of years, grown men and women have believed in scenarios of a similar nature to the one I have just described, but information has been passed down from generation to generation, and has become part of the collective unconscious. Questioning the truth of this information has been strongly discouraged. No longer, thankfully, are people forced to hear this so-called truth, or frightened into believing it. Over the generations many new ideas have evolved. God isn't nearly so frightening as he must have seemed hundreds of years ago. Churches are changing, and yet many of the ideas in the scenario I created above, remain firmly intact.

It's difficult to imagine this in such a modern society, and yet it never ceases to amaze me what people do still believe, and are still being taught.

There are also many people who simply cannot believe what seems to them a fairy story, and yet they know that there is something out there. They sort of believe in God, but not the traditional scenario. They are not really sure what God is, or isn't. They sort of want to know but don't want religion. They like the idea of someone or something watching over us all, but, well, you know how it is.

Over the last twelve years I have been privileged to a great deal of information that has changed my perception of the exact nature of God. For those of you who would like to consider something new, I'd like to share what I know.

I have always referred to God as, 'my heavenly father'. This goes back to my days at church. I still refer to God as my heavenly father, as a mark of respect, and because I guess I'm used to it. It feels comfortable to refer to the creator as Father. The Lord encouraged us to refer to God as our father, our creator the one who gave us life. 'Father' helps to give our human minds a way to connect, to bond with God. In reality God is androgynous, a perfect balance of masculine and feminine energy, our creator is both mother and father. This isn't a feminist thing. Bear with me!

It is my personal belief that the reason the Lord referred to God as merely father was because, he was wise enough to recognise that a male-dominated society, such as he walked among, would find it too difficult to accept God as part female, let alone understand androgyny. The reality of what and who God is was not as important at that time, as the spiritual message that he was sent among the people to teach.

Therefore, to help create a bond with the creator, an understanding of God from a human perspective, at a level of understanding at that time, was a more diplomatic way of teaching the people the higher truth. As our hearts and minds become more open and receptive to the truth and when we are prepared to put aside preconceived ideas, then more of the truth can be given to us.

God is a loving intelligence, present within and surrounding every single thing in the universe! Nothing in the universe can exist without God. In effect everything is God, or at least a part of God. Everything that we are, everything that we have, everything that is, has been created from the energy that is the loving intelligence we know as God. A chair may appear to be a solid inanimate object, but in fact it is energy; molecules, atoms vibrating at a very slow rate, in order for it to appear solid and tangible. We are the same; energy, vibrating at a slower rate, in order that we may experience physical senses. Since we are made of the same loving intelligence energy known as God, it is safe to say that we are all part of God. It becomes easier to understand that God dwells within us, as well as all around us. It also is easier to understand how God can be all-seeing and all-knowing, and how he can understand you and your needs so well. God isn't on some throne in the sky. He is with you, always, here on earth.

A personal lesson in realising just how connected we are to God, how much we are a part of God, and he a part of us, came to me one day when I was feeling particularly sorry for myself, and feeling like a complete failure, as though I was letting God down.

I felt I was missing the point, not absorbing spiritual lessons fast enough, plus a thousand other negative things, so ridiculous, I can't even remember now. You may have been there too! Anyway, I was feeling pretty low. Whilst I did the washing up, I blabbed on to God until I was all cried out. Then I started to calm down and finished my prayer. I felt a little better by then, because I knew my prayer would be answered. Somehow I knew that God wouldn't think I was as bad as all that, and more importantly wouldn't say, 'Pull yourself together and try harder next time.' Knowing that made me feel better straight away. I knew I was being particularly hard on myself, but as I began the process of being a bit kinder to myself, I could hear a song playing in my mind. The song was, *The Wind Beneath My Wings*.

I didn't have a copy of that song at the time, so the only words I thought I knew, were snatches that I'd heard on the radio. But obviously my subconscious mind had stored much more than I realised. As the words floated gently through my mind, a very powerful message started to come through to me along with an overwhelming feeling of love. I felt cherished.

Just in case you are not familiar with the words of the song I have written them down below.

The Wind Beneath My Wings

It must have been cold there in my shadow, to never have sunlight on your face,
You've been content to let me shine; you always walked a step behind,
I was the one with all the glory, while you were the one with all the strength,
Only a face without a name, I never once heard you complain,
Did you ever know that you're my hero, and everything I would like to be?
See I can fly higher than an eagle, you are the wind beneath my wings,
It might have appeared to go unnoticed, but I've got it all here in my heart,
I want you to know, I know the truth, I would be nothing without you,
Did you ever know that you're my hero, and everything I would like to be?
See I can fly higher than an eagle, you are the wind beneath my wings.

As this beautiful song unfolded, I realised that God was telling me how precious I was in his eyes. The song interpreted his feelings about me, and each one of us, in this way.

You must have been very lonely there in the negative energy that you allowed to surround you, cutting yourself off from the light and my love.

You've been content to let me shine in your life, and yet you do not allow yourself to shine by being happy, to experience joy, and self worth. You give me all the glory, yet you are the one with all the strength. It takes a lot of courage to leave the heavenly realms and live on earth, to walk an unconventional path, to learn, to experience.

When it got to the bit that said, 'Did you ever know that you're my hero, and everything I'd like to be? See I can fly higher than an eagle, you are the wind beneath my wings', I realised that God was telling me we are all players in his play, the world is our stage, and we are all the heroes with different parts to play. God is almighty, of that there can be no doubt, but he needs us to give him expression. Without me, and everyone of us, every creature, plant, every creation, God cannot be expressed. God the almighty is also humble enough to recognise little insignificant me as important to him. He knows he needs you and me, in order to be more than just a loving intelligent energy.

'It might have appeared to go unnoticed, but I've got it all here in my heart, I want you to know I know the truth, I would be nothing without you.'

It might not seem obvious to me, but God has recorded everything that I am or ever will be. He won't forget and wanted me to know that the truth is, 'I am nothing without you my precious one.'

In his heart God wants me to know that he recognised how important we all are. Each one of us doing our bit for God and God is grateful, God loves us. I began to feel I'm not a failure after all, not in God's eyes. When I started thinking more positively, I realised, yes I'm not doing so badly. I'm actually trying very hard, I've actually learned a great deal, and I've come a long way. As I started thinking more kindly about myself, I realised I was beginning to understand more about who and what God really is!

I am part of God, part of God is me. I need God to exist, but God also needs me to help in his expression. We are a team. We are all part of God; we are all part of the whole, that is God.

I don't know about you, but I haven't heard of many people just lately who have heard God talking to them from behind a burning bush! Most people won't see God coming out of the sky and standing in front of them. I'm not saying it couldn't happen, it's just that for most of us God is more subtle, and creative. Did I say subtle? Well maybe not all the time! For example, God will often speak to me through music, as I have just described. I love music and singing, so music is a very natural medium for God to use.

But answers do not come to me through music all the time. For instance, once when I asked for the answer to something, I waited for the reply to come to me, but it didn't come straight away, as is often the case. I knew I'd get an answer in time, and I did. I was in the library, looking at a book, when suddenly one fell off the shelf above, straight on to my head. As I read the title, I knew that I would find my answer in that very book! 'Thanks,' I said looking upward. Perhaps I should also have said, 'Remind me to take a crash helmet next time.' Why do I look up when I talk to God, when I know God is within me and all around me as well? Old habit I guess. Besides if God is all around then he's also above as well, isn't he? Anyway I digress; but what I'm trying to say is that God will answer your prayers in many different ways, sometimes subtly sometimes not, sometimes instantly, sometimes you may have to wait a while. He is very creative, and knows how best to reach you to inspire you, to touch your heart, to help you.

For example the stranger you met at the bus stop on the day your car broke down, and you cursed, because buses are so inconvenient, aren't they? But then you did say, 'God if you're listening I really need a job badly, can you help?' The stranger you began talking to just happens to be very influential at the office where there is an ideal career for you, etcetera... God doesn't do things by halves, no ordinary job for you, to tide you over, unless you can benefit in some way from a temporary job. But let's not get too deep I'm sure you get the picture.

Sometimes you won't even realise that your prayer is being

answered until say a couple of months or even years down the line. You may not even have said a prayer in the conventional sense, but remember, God is within you, and knows all of your heart's desires, needs etcetera. You are sending out signals to the universe all the time. This is important. Are your signals positive, creative, self-believing, do you have self-esteem? Or are you someone who says things like, 'I'll never get a job, I'm too old, inexperienced, etcetera.' What about, 'Dear God please will you help me get a job? I'm in trouble with the bank; please please help, amen.' Then two minutes later make a statement like, 'I don't suppose God will help me. I'm no saint. Or, why should God help me? I only go to church when there is a wedding in the family,' and so on and so forth. Well that's all right with God. He loves you anyway. He always wants to help you. He's not worried about how many times you go to church. But he is concerned that you asked for his help then immediately dismissed him as a crazy idea. He's concerned about your self-esteem; you're shutting him out. In that moment you're own negative thoughts and feelings became an energy block against the creative light that is God within you.

As you continue to think negatively, so you send out more negative energy into the universe, and like a boomerang it comes back to you. In other words, your troubles get worse. And where was God when you needed him most? Always there with you, ready and willing to help you. Concerned that you chose negativity to work with, to create your world, instead of positive energy to create a better world for yourself. God gave you free will in order that you might choose for yourself. What would you learn if it were all done for you? If it were forced upon you, if you had no say? What's the point of trying to teach a person how to ride a bike, if you never allow them to get on the bike and try for themselves? Maybe they will fall off a few times, choose a bumpy road, when a smooth one is next to them, but you have to let them find out for themselves.

Be prepared to let go of preconceived ideas about how you want God to answer your prayer. Be flexible. In this way you allow God to effect a much better solution. I have found that he has a way of coming up with things which you might never have imagined in a million years!

A lot of people are afraid to ask God for help for themselves because it is considered selfish to ask for something for ourselves, especially when others are worse off than perhaps we are. Our universe is a universe of infinite abundance. We all have only to accept all that God has to offer. People are also afraid to ask God about things that may not seem to be very spiritual. For instance some might think it improper to approach God regarding the subject of sex. Or perhaps something is worrying you that may be considered too trivial to put to God.

I once spoke to God about something that was upsetting me. I was afraid to talk to anyone else in case I was laughed at. I told God that I realised my concerns may seem rather trivial, but it was upsetting me. God's reply to me was, 'Heather if it concerns you, then it concerns me. Therefore it is important to me.' From that day on I knew that I need never be afraid to share anything with God.

However you see God, whether as a biblical figure or universal energy, God is still there for you, watching, waiting, ready to help you get the best from life. You don't have to go to church unless you want to, but if you want your world, your tomorrow to be better than perhaps it is now, you need to use your creative energy (your God energy) in a positive way today. By choosing to express such positive attributes as kindness, generosity and understanding (and most important don't forget to be kind to yourself as well as others). Let creativity within you shine and bring out your self-esteem. Be happy, joyful, non-judgemental. You make up the rest. You know where I am coming from. All energy is God. You decide if God will be expressed positively or negatively.

God is perfect love seeking expression in the physical world. You and me, we are all part of God, an expression of God manifested on earth. So that perfect love may be expressed through you and me. Not by force, of course; freewill gives us the right to choose.

If we are part of God, what does that make us? Many facets of love! God on earth as yet not fully realised. Now all we have to do is realise it!

Chapter Five

PRE-EXISTENCE

HOW DO YOU WRITE ABOUT A SUBJECT THAT IS BEYOND OUR normal comprehension? I asked the top man for spiritual guidance, as I have done with every chapter I have written. 'I want to understand the soul's journey,' I said, 'I want to understand how we evolve. Do we reincarnate and, if we do, how do we?'

And so I went on, after many prayers and me going on, why this, how that... please tell me the truth, the whole truth! Then one day I felt a voice inside my head, telling me to take up a pen and paper, then sit down quietly. Maybe this is it! I thought. They are going to dictate to me! Instead I was asked to close my eyes and draw a rose. So I began, with my eyes closed, to draw, to the best of my ability, a rosebud. First I drew the petals, then the frilly bit that cups the petals, then a stem, and leaves, I even gave it thorns and veins. I wanted to give it as much detail as possible. When I looked at what I had drawn, I wasn't surprised to see it was disjointed, but you could see it was a rosebud, the stem didn't join with the bud, the leaves were in the wrong place, the thorns overlapped. The rest was a bit jumbled, still, considering I couldn't see. It wasn't too bad, you could make it out. Whilst I was wondering what this all had to do with the writing of my book, I heard the voice in my head say, 'Now Heather it's a pink rose.' Try describing pink to someone who has never seen pink before?

I went through the rest of the day trying to describe pink, with words like soft, gentle, tender, candy floss, baby soft... but nothing I thought of really could describe pink. You try it! Defeated, I realised that what I was being told, was that something from a multidimensional world was too difficult to really explain in its truest sense, to someone in the three-dimensional world, like me, who has no conscious memory or concept of what it is all like, (not to mention that I'm no Einstein!).

So at best, what I have to offer is the best of my ability to convey the truth. Albeit a bit disjointed, crude, simplistic and colourless. Perhaps one day I will realise the magnitude of what I was asking the Lord, I can almost see him shaking his head and saying, 'Oh no Heather not that question, my dear, please!'

When that frenzied moment, after the pushing has stopped, when the midwife announces, 'It's a girl,' and you take your first gasp of air, and holler at the top of your lungs that you are not happy to be here, taken out of your peaceful watery home, to arrive where? Here? The disinfectant and other unfamiliar smells and feelings, all the adults crying, laughing, oohing and aahing. The bewilderment as you are placed in the arms of Mum? What time is it, 2.30 a.m.? Isn't she wonderful, just two minutes old, and not a care in the world, not a care? What! I've got news for you mum. I'm older than you can possibly imagine. And as for cares in the world, I've had my share; this isn't my first time here you know. Don't you remember, we arranged all this long ago! I must say I rather hoped re-entry might have been better this time around. Still can't be helped, I'm here now anyway, so let's begin, I think I'll start by having another nap, and if you are wise you'll do the same mum. Hard work this life business!

Pre-Existence

The divine spark, or spirit, given to each soul is an aspect of God. A chip off the old block, if you like. A moment in time, when each soul became consciousness. God's consciousness in action. In other words, our souls became God's expression, actively, born of a desire to explore consciousness in physical form. Maybe this is where the concept of man made in God's image comes from, and why the misconception that God is a human being, albeit divine, began. We are made of God's energy, light, and consciousness. Like balls of light that appear to be separate from God, and yet we are not, since everything we are whether we are on earth or in Heaven is made of God. God is therefore omnipresent, in us and all around us, *is* us. We are a part of God and apart from God at the same time.

Twin Souls

God's energy is androgynous. That is to say a perfect balance of masculine and feminine energy. During the evolutionary process the androgynous soul splits its consciousness in two, to become two individual souls, one to be a more masculine aspect, the other a more feminine aspect. Although in reality both aspects are created of androgynous energy and therefore always carry both masculine and feminine energy. Both aspects are now individual souls in their own right, who happen to share exactly the same vibrational note.

Because these two aspects or souls share the same vibration, they are naturally attracted to each other, like magnets. Since androgyny is the natural state, the desire to come back together as one is strong and powerful, all compelling. However in order to experience physical life and to interact, separation of these two magnets is necessary, in order that life can be experienced from both the masculine and the feminine perspective. Therefore both the male and female souls pair off with new soulmates, with different but compatible vibrations. This allows interaction rather than complete mergence. However the two original twin souls never lost contact with each other. A constant stream of conscious energy is flowing between them; (on earth this is usually subconscious). When twin soul energies come together, they become androgynous again. That is to say they blend mind to mind. Except that once the twin souls have experienced life on earth, and start to evolve, they have become individual intelligences in their own right. However these two intelligences are so naturally in tune with each other that they can and do blend their two individual intelligences completely, to become one intelligence, when working together, and sharing experiences. Yet still they retain their individuality.

Twin souls do not always evolve at the same rate, once they become individual. They evolve at an individual rate, and they have individual choice and free will. However the twin soul's vibrational contact is constant at higher self level, and each twin has access to the other twin's memories and experiences, whether this is consciously perceived or not. If these two have made contact on earth, then psychic and telepathic awareness may increase. Then it can be like two people sharing an ethereal phone line.

The purpose of the twin soul is that each androgynous essence should experience the masculine and feminine principles, and interactions of life from both perspectives. The split allows contrast. Unfortunately a lot of airy fairy new age romantic misconceptions is propounded about twin souls, suggesting that twin souls have become lost and separated over the aeons of time, and it is our purpose in life to search for our one and only true mate, in order to find true happiness and fulfilment. This could not be further from the truth, not to mention the damage so called 'twin soul reunions' have caused to otherwise perfectly good marriages.

Twin souls are never lost, can and do always know how to find each other, at least in spirit. So the chance of you meeting and spending time together, in spirit at least, is fairly high. Twin souls do not often incarnate at the same time, or if they do, do not usually meet, as the meeting is like two magnets. It is a bit of a wrench for twin souls to be separated, as there is a natural affinity. Also interaction with each other for long periods of time would result in little evolutionary gain. Therefore, usually twin souls do not come together to marry or share other intimate relationships. Having said that, they can incarnate close to each other, perhaps to work together, usually for a spiritual purpose. Perhaps their two energies together will create the more powerful vibration needed to fulfil a spiritual mission, or maybe these two will come together to help their twin with a particular lesson that they may be having difficulties with. Marriage between these two isn't impossible or out of the question, it's just rare.

When these two energies do come together it is pretty dynamic and powerful, as when these minds work together, it is more a case of 'you and me we are three'. Two individual intelligences and one androgynous intelligence. Not only that, but on the exact vibration. A very powerful force. A great deal of good is potentially possible, providing both souls have evolved to high enough standards. But unlike the mythical romance of twin souls who are always loving, romantic, perfect partners, the reality is that from a soul level, these two maybe resonating in perfect harmony. But the very human qualities that each soul is experiencing, while on earth, despite the natural soul affinity and bond between the twin souls, means that their personalities can still clash. If twin souls are working on the lower levels of consciousness, they can hurt each other, just as any other soul can hurt another, but the pain will be more deeply felt. This is another good reason perhaps for keeping these two apart on earth, at least until they have evolved enough. Make no mistake, meeting your twin soul will not necessarily guarantee marital bliss, as has been suggested, but it can be a very rich and special relationship if you are lucky enough to meet and work with them. Don't go looking for them. If you are meant to meet you can be sure you will, as it will be written into your incarnational experience. In other words it is predestined!

Soul Mates

Soul mates have always been associated with love, romance, marriage and star-crossed lovers. Information written on the subject often overlaps with that of the twin soul and the idea that opposites attract like a magnet. Because of our love affair with this romantic idea, it is easy to see how we have focused our idea of soul mate as being one and the same as twin souls. A romantic, ideal partner, who one day we will meet and live with happily ever after.

The truth is that unlike twin souls, that we only have one of, and are always the opposite sex to us, soul mates are both sexes, and we have many. We can meet them in all aspects of our life. They can be a parent, a best friend, a colleague at work, a teacher, or a nurse. And of course they can be a lover, a marriage partner or even a brief but meaningful encounter. Soul mates are souls that we have agreed to meet and work with on earth; (we may also work with them in the spirit world). We work together to learn, to teach. Maybe we can work on a project together, perhaps for the higher good of our community etcetera. Of course we maybe meeting a soul mate that we have met and worked with many times before. Perhaps we have a lot of karmic links to a certain soul, and we keep coming to earth, to try to correct a situation between us, heal and balance a wrong, finish some unfinished business that we started in a previous life. Karmic bonds are now famously connected with soul mates, but they may not be the romantic stuff that romantic novels are made of. Some of these soul mates that we have karmic bonds with, can lead to some gritty situations during the learning process.

With a soul mate there is often a sense of knowing the person, or a feeling of instant rapport, even though you may never have met on earth in this incarnation. You chat away like old friends. But sometimes there can be a feeling of instant dislike, even though you have never met. Of course, we will always like or dislike some people more than others, but this is a different feeling; deeper, more intense, lasting, you could even say soul-deep. Sometimes there will be things that need to be worked out between two or more souls that are reflected by feelings of animosity.

Soul mates come in all shapes and sizes, not just the variety of star-crossed lovers across a crowded room.

Predestination

A divine plan created by God, in which each of us would have our own part to play. Not only are we united in a common goal, but also each one of us has an individual goal to work towards. This goal when successfully reached, is our personal contribution toward the larger divine plan. A privilege and honour creating inside of each one of us a compelling desire to complete and successfully fulfil. Therefore each one of us with help and guidance from higher wisdom, has created a personal plan of action to be worked through on earth, in order to learn all that we need, that we might fulfil our spiritual mission and personal contribution. For many souls there would be a need for many earthly incarnations, in order to perfect skills, increase knowledge, wisdom and understanding of the many facets of love; not to mention the mistakes that would be inevitable as part of the learning process, that would need to be healed and corrected.

Before you came to earth you planned your trip so to speak;

you already knew your spiritual mission and what you wanted to accomplish. The next thing then was to work out the best plan of action. I don't know how this was achieved in the early days of our evolution, but I do know that spiritual masters, and those who have been assigned to be our spiritual guides, of whom there could be more than one, give higher wisdom. I know that I have a personal team of seven spiritual guides, at least that's how many I saw on the day that they graciously showed themselves to me. I guess God thought that this one is going to be a handful, better give her seven spiritual guides, I do ask a lot of questions! But seriously, each soul is assigned spiritual guidance according to the personal needs and skills that they need to develop.

Between you, your spiritual guides, and higher wisdom still, your plan of action is worked out in agreement with those other souls who will play a part in your plan, whilst also, at the same time you can play an important role in the plan of each of these souls, whose lives you will touch in a large or small way. The majority of souls who will become your earth family, close friends, teachers, work colleagues, lovers etcetera are part of your soul group, and you have met many times before, throughout your personal history of incarnation. These souls you have the most affinity with, at soul level. These souls will play major roles in your life, as will you in their lives. Each of us has something valuable to offer to the life experience of each person we meet, and of course during our lifetime there will be many people that we will meet, and interact with; some long term, some brief encounters.

Because it is not just your plan, but their personal plans that have to be taken into account, you begin to understand what a complex situation you are involved in. Your plan is worked out to the finest detail, from your parents, the work you need to become engaged in, your race, religious background, whether from a rich or poor family. This is set against the backdrop of all the experiences you have already gained in previous lifetimes. There is negative energy still held within your soul energy field, as yet unhealed, that assures that like attracts like. The negative energy that you will attract offers opportunities to learn and heal. Once healed they no longer stay within your energy field and therefore you no longer attract the same negative lesson (I will go into this in greater detail later). I have only touched briefly on the things that have to be worked out before we come to earth, but you can see how complicated it all is. How meticulously fine-tuned our plans need to be; and that includes your entry into the world, as transiting influences all play their part, the time line, historical events, collective consciousness, attitudes, prejudices etcetera. Were you born prematurely? Don't worry you were meant to be!

Free Will

Free will has been given to us in order that we might come to an understanding of love through our own volition. Experience will give us that understanding, but experience by force is little more than going through the motions, whereas experience with choice is a true learning experience. By its very nature, love cannot be forced upon us, therefore free will and predestination go hand in hand.

We have always had free will, but it is by your actions and reaction that you yourself create your own restrictions. To have complete free will, is to be free of hang-ups, bad attitudes, old hurts, prejudice, fears etcetera. It is these very things that compel us to seek a destiny that calls upon us to confront our faults and failings, in order that we might experience true free will in all things. There are times when we are forced to endure difficulties. It is not a punishment. We know that the faults and failings within us will inevitably attract similar back to us. This is because we are all subject to the law of cause and effect. We therefore choose lessons and opportunities to set ourselves free from the restrictions and limits imposed by our faults and failings.

Because of the level of consciousness that we are operating on, the lessons are often hard, uncomfortable, and painful; for example: perhaps you have a colour prejudice, that is mainly dormant within you. You live happily in your community predominated by one ethnic group, when one day your world is turned upside down, because your job is relocated to a multi-cultured community. Suddenly all your prejudices come to the fore. You know that you must go. Your responsibility to your family and their needs is so strong within you. Perhaps you vow it will only be for a while, and maybe it will, but how will you deal with the new situation that you are faced with. Continued resentment, suspicion and rudeness? Or do you take the opportunity to get to know some of these people. Offer the hand of friendship, even though it might be hard and strange for you at first. Is your mind open to this new experience? Or are you just going through the motions, saying in a self-righteous way, 'I tried to offer the hand of friendship – it wasn't my fault; I knew he'd be like that, his kind always are.' It is predestined that you will face this situation, meet these souls who wear the guise of a different race. You helped set it up, but now that the time has come, you can choose how you will respond within this situation. You can create any number of realities for yourself. Will you choose positive or negative? If you choose to be positive you will never have to create a situation like that again. You have overcome and dissolved your prejudice.

Since like attracts like you will continue to draw toward you whatever you give out. In other words if you keep thinking negatively, you will continue to attract negative lessons to yourself. Until you change to a higher level of consciousness, you cannot expect the reality you live to get any better.

It is wise to remember that your thoughts create your future reality. When we keep thinking in a certain way, we are programming our subconscious mind. In this way we are taken unawares. You may ask yourself, 'Why has this terrible thing happened to me; what have I done to deserve this?' The chances are you can trace it back to your attitudes, or fears. The things you constantly say, 'I knew this was going to happen, didn't I keep saying something like this would happen?' Of course it will eventually, because you kept programming it in to your subconscious mind, and then like attracts like. By thinking in a more positive way, by being thoughtful about what we say and think, we can attract much more happiness and joy into our lives, instead of so much pain and suffering. Pain and suffering can help us to grow a great deal. If we can learn to transcend the resentment that builds up around the pain and suffering. But why take the hard road when the easier road offers us many more lessons through joy and happiness.

A negative mind is a mind cut off from God, and higher

assistance. I'm not talking about the religious God. Not being a churchgoer doesn't make you a negative person. I'm talking about the God within each and everyone of us. Whether you acknowledge God or not, by being open minded, open hearted and positive you are more in touch with your feelings and intuition. Whatever you call it, get in touch with that still, small voice within you. Act upon the advice, the warnings. Learn to balance your logical mind with your intuitive mind. I know we live in a world where science and fact seem to rule, but both faculties need to be developed and appreciated. If we didn't need both, we wouldn't have both. You may have to be patient with intuitive feelings for a while. If you have neglected to listen to them, you will have to re-learn the art of feeling again.

I wish I had listened when I was nineteen years old, the night I met my former husband. My friend diplomatically got out of the car, and went indoors leaving us alone. Then it happened; he asked me out, I had hoped he would. But then I heard a voice loud in my ear, 'Don't go with him.' I'll never forget it. It was so loud and clear that I hesitated for a while. It was as if someone was in the car on the back seat, but my friend had already left the car. My husband-to-be saw my hesitation and thought I wasn't interested. With his pride injured, he said, 'Well you don't have to, make your mind up.' I saw he was hurt, so I said, 'No, of course I'd like to.' From that moment on my fate was sealed, so to speak. My spiritual guide could do no more for the moment. He had advised me and I exercised my free will. I often wonder if my guide sighed and, shaking his head, said, 'Teenagers, will they ever listen?' Well, not listening, caused me a lot of heartache. Yes, we married, but it wasn't part of my destiny. We had little in common, and sixteen months after we exchanged vows, it was over. The marriage, that was, not my heartache. The pain was dreadful. The silly thing is that it wasn't meant to be. If I had only listened, I needn't have suffered like I did. Having said that, I know that the experience has helped me to grow spiritually, and so I wouldn't change a thing, but I think I'd rather listen and skip the pain next time and let learning be a happier experience.

So what happens when we stray off the path? Do we loose out on opportunities? Well, yes and no. That is to say that, opportunities can be lost, but similar opportunities will be set up at a later date. The plan is not ruled by linear time, neither is it inflexible. Every time we exercise our free will in a way that is detrimental to our spiritual well-being, the plan has to be altered, I don't know how this is done exactly, but I do know that a lot is accomplished during sleep state, when we astral travel to the spirit world. If we are really off-track, then our spiritual guides have to take what emergency measures they can. They always have contact with our higher self, even if we seem to have lost contact, and are not listening. Our higher self is our soul self, within us and without us at the same time. We are multidimensional souls, which is why our spiritual guides can consult our higher self, even if we are not listening. But let's not get side tracked at the moment.

Your higher self is the part of you that knows your plan and the best course of action. It's the part of you that makes you feel good and centred when you are doing the right thing. This may not be what everyone else wants you to do, or even what you've been taught to be the right thing. Your higher self does not fit into neat little boxes. When you feel anxious, restless and confused you can be sure you are not in touch with your higher self. It is the part of you that says I want to leave my job in insurance and get into botany. That's where I will be happiest. But, then logic stops you from following your heart because insurance is safe. But your higher self is pleading, and your heart will never be happy until you find the courage to try botany. It doesn't mean behave in an irresponsible way, and forget your obligations and responsibilities. But once you really make your mind up, then it's your higher self and your spiritual guides who lead you to your lucky breaks, and things just seem to flow and fall into place. When you are banging your head against a brick wall (metaphorically speaking) because obstacles are in your way, this is probably because something isn't right for you. Your higher wisdom is trying to protect you. Maybe it's not that it isn't right for you, but that there is a better way to it, or the timing isn't right just yet. If you persist, things become frustrating and you feel exhausted, and worn out. That isn't to say you should give up, but maybe take a break, look at things from a different angle, let go, relax, sleep on it, lots of answers come to us after we have slept. That is because we've travelled astrally to seek help. Getting in touch with your higher self isn't easy at first, since we've been out of practice too long, but learning to relax and let go of the problem for a while is a good place to start. Take notice of the feelings that go with your thoughts. I cannot give you a formula. Everybody's way is different. You have to find the best way for you. I use music to calm me, or I go for a walk alone. Also I use prayer. Sometimes I am better at making contact with my higher self than others. I'm still learning, but it's always worth the effort.

Of course, no matter how good we may be at listening to higher wisdom and acting on the advice, we can never have guarantees that things will go exactly according to plan, simply because everybody has free will and will make their own choices. Everyone is evolving at his or her own rate. Everyone has their own hang-ups, fears, gripes and issues to deal with. Obviously the more positive, kind, open-hearted, generous, tolerant, patient and so on, we are with those we come into contact with, the better the situation will turn out in the end. If something is right for you, a way will be found.

Are you one who always gives your power away? Do you let others choose for you? Do you often find yourself in situations where you have no choice? Do you allow fear to limit your choice? The chances are you do. We all do from time to time, but when we do this, we give our power away. How weak willed are you? Do you always give in because you don't want to upset the other person? Do you always say yes, even though you'd rather say no? Do you change your plans to accommodate someone, even though they never do the same for you and, instead, allow yourself to be manipulated? Perhaps you are afraid that they will think you mean, selfish or unkind. Of course we should do kind generous things for each other. Of course we should be helpful, share our talents and knowledge, and give whenever we can. But if your heart isn't in it, then you are just going through the motions. If you resent what you are doing then you will not be doing yourself any favours. We all need to learn to respect and honour ourselves as well as all those we meet and share our lives with. If you offer your advice, help and opinion and it is rejected, do you respect that person's right to choose, or do you sulk, turn your back, tell them not to ask for your help again.

Power isn't about beating the other person, or getting one over on them, but about being able to recognise when backing down, and retreating are preferable, at least until a better approach can be tried. Yes, the other person might behave in a smug self-righteous way, and think they have won, but smug self-righteousness isn't power either. Love and love of yourself, giving yourself time to think things out calmly, compromise balance. This is power; working out a way that will not hurt another or infringe on their right to choose, of course!

Of course, saying these things is one thing, but the practice is more difficult. That isn't to say we should give up trying, but neither should we expect ourselves to be perfect. As we walk our way, step-by-step through the complex game of life, it is inevitable that we will make mistakes. The important thing to remember is our intentions. For, when the time comes for us to review our life on earth, we can see just how much, or how little, we have accomplished, how much time was wasted on petty things, how many things we left unaccomplished, and how foolish behaviour deprives us of successfully completing our spiritual mission; the one that we so wanted to complete. We can see not only how much we have left undone, unlearned, but how much damage we have done and how much we shall need to put right on our next visit to earth. Of course we shall also see how much we have accomplished. How much we won't have to do again. How much we have helped others. Just what we did contribute and leave for those we left behind.

After the life review, and a long rest, we get ready to start out again to continue with our life plan, using our past experiences to hopefully improve, correct, heal, and progress. This journey is known as reincarnation, but that is another story. For now I'd like to share a personal story with you that reinforces my belief in predestination.

Lucy

Lucy came to me for reflexology, but very quickly we became friends. Lucy who is a computer consultant, helped me to obtain the PC with which I am now typing this book. She and her husband, John, have been very generous with their time and expertise in helping me to learn how to use it.

Quite early on in our friendship both Lucy and I felt that somehow we were meant to meet, and that this was predestined. Our feelings were to prove right, but not for the reasons we both thought. Although the computer was a godsend, fate had brought us together for a different purpose. Lucy had been having trouble conceiving when she first came to me, but happily in March of this year (2000) Lucy became pregnant. Her baby was due in November. Of course I was happy for her, but didn't think much about it. Then one day in July, a very hot day, Lucy arrived to give me some more help on the computer. She had her hair up in a ponytail. When I opened the door I gasped, 'It's you!' Poor Lucy looked at me, confused, and said, 'You are expecting me, aren't you?' I let her in and started to explain. 'I didn't recognise you before, but with your hair up like that I do. I've seen you before in a dream I had about four years ago.' It was so clear that I've never forgotten it. I began to explain the dream to her. How I had been in the spirit world talking to a spiritual guide and she showed me an image of a girl, who was heavily pregnant. She had her hair up, 'Just like you do today,' I told Lucy. I was also shown images of the girl being taken to hospital, in a car, and being helped into the hospital. The guide told me March to November, and, 'Not to worry, Heather, it's all been arranged.' That's all I could remember when I woke up. But it was so powerful I had never forgotten it, although I didn't understand it. I could never work out who the girl in the dream was until then. We both hugged each other and laughed. 'There you are,' Lucy said, 'I knew we were meant to meet.' I agreed.

We were still convinced it was to do with the computer and my book and that was the meaning of, 'it's been arranged'.

But there was to be more to come. I could never have imagined in a million years, what was going to happen next!

A couple of weeks later my husband and I invited Lucy and John over to dinner, as a little thank-you for all of their kind help with the computer.

Whilst we were eating, Lucy stopped and said, 'Heather I've got something to ask you. I don't know how you will feel about this, but, John and I have talked it all through and we would like to employ you to be present when I go in to have the baby. I'd like you to perform reflexology and healing to help calm me down.'

I was so overcome with feelings of honour and privilege, I had to go upstairs and compose myself for a minute. Having never had children of my own, I was filled with so many emotions all at once; I was overwhelmed. I wasn't sure just how long they wanted me to be there for, so very gently I tried to clarify just at what point did they want me to leave. After all I didn't want to invade their privacy at that very special moment.

But Lucy was adamant. 'So long as you'd like to stay Heather we'd both like you to be there right to the end, if you want to.'

At the time of writing this Lucy had about four weeks to go. We all agreed that at anytime if either of them wanted me to leave, or if I wanted to leave, we would speak up and respect each other's wishes, as this would be too special a moment to cause any tension. But somehow I knew I would be there to see this soul make his or her entrance into the world because I've been told, 'Don't worry Heather it's all been arranged!'

Lucy had a little boy and I was privileged to be present. I worked hard for twelve hours, not as hard as Lucy did of course, and I got home exhausted, but exhilarated. What an amazing experience! One I shall cherish all of my life. For those of you who are interested in astrology, I looked up the natal chart planet positions of the baby, and compared them with the positions on my natal chart. I shouldn't have been surprised, but was absolutely astonished to find aspects in our charts matching up to the exact degree, where his birth and my work are concerned. Suffice to say that my findings increased my belief that things really are very precisely worked out in advance!

Chapter Six

ABORTION

S O MUCH PAIN, ANGUISH, GUILT, AND FEAR SURROUND AN abortion. There can be very few, who have chosen to take such a step, without going through some, if not all of these, and similar emotions; often wishing the clock could be turned back. Wondering who will support you and, worse, who will condemn you. Whether in a secure relationship, or not, whatever a woman's personal reasons to abort, it is unlikely to be a decision that is taken lightly. It is a huge responsibility and a heavy burden to carry. Carried alone, or shared, it is doubtful that your final decision will please everyone you tell, whether family or friends. As if this is not enough, there is the trauma of the aftermath. If you go ahead with an abortion, there will be the questions. Did I do the right thing? Did I make the wrong decision; will I go to hell? Have I done something unforgivable? Am I wicked? Have I committed murder or taken a life? How long will Auntie Freda shut me out, condemn me or bring up the subject, at every family gathering? Can't she see I did what I thought was best?

Abortion can haunt you for many years, festering away at the subconscious. These pains, if left unhealed, will often manifest themselves in later life, as a disease of the physical body, or deep psychological scars, that hinder our souls' evolutionary progress. Such pain and torment must be healed. The way to do this is through self-love and forgiveness. But how will we ever forgive and love ourselves, when we are brought up to believe for example that abortion is wicked or that we may be subjected to hellfire and brimstone for our sins. Most of us know these days, that this isn't likely to happen. But ingrained into our subconscious are a lot of misguided belief systems, which keep us firmly entrenched in fear, doubt and uncertainty. Just what will happen to us?

It's time that we knew the truth, so that we can heal and move on in our journey back to God, love and the divine.

It may be helpful to know that the Auntie Fredas of this world are on a spiritual journey as well. She still has a lot to learn. A decision to have an abortion will bring Auntie Freda the opportunity to learn such things as compassion, tolerance, forgiveness etcetera. Also she can learn how to let go of control. Every time you exercise your free will, and choose something that doesn't suit Auntie Freda, she becomes upset, and tries to manipulate you. In this way she is the one who has violated the spiritual law of love, not you. She has forgotten to honour your right to free will and freedom of choice, which God has given to us all. She then judges you because you do not do her will. Her weapon is to withdraw her love from you, in the hope that you will see things her way. She has also seen your situation from her point of view, with her current circumstances, and belief system.

There is a saying, 'never judge a man until you have walked a mile in his moccasins'. In other words Auntie Freda forgets, it's impossible to judge fairly, unless you understand completely. But rather than treat Auntie Freda as the villain of the peace, we should try to be patient, perhaps send loving thoughts and kindness her way, in the hope that soon she will learn a very valuable lesson.

It would help us all including Auntie Freda, if we understood the spiritual truth behind abortion!

Will God judge you, as Auntie Freda does? No of course not. God never forgets the gift of free will he has bestowed upon all men and women. Is God cross with you? Will he turn his back on you because you chose to have an abortion? That may be a human characteristic, but it is not a characteristic of God, who is love. Whether you choose an abortion or not, you will find that both choices are filled with opportunity for spiritual growth, for you, and all others around you. Therefore Heaven does not judge your choice, your decision, as either good or bad, but as a choice of opportunity for spiritual growth. Since Heaven has a much broader view of the picture, there is no need to judge. Judgement is a human characteristic.

Now what about the poor soul that was about to embark on its spiritual journey to earth? Has that soul lost its opportunity? Does God care? Of course God cares, but still he does not judge. His broader perspective means that he understands everything about us individually and as a whole, he understands what we are going through, our needs, our beliefs and limitations. He knows how far we have advanced on our spiritual journey. He also understands about the incoming or aborted soul, their birth plan, and what they will need in order to carry it through to success.

God is complete and unconditional love. Through God all things are possible. God's divine plan is flexible. It has to be, in order to accommodate the free will that he has given to us. Therefore if abortion is to take place, new plans, if needed, can be set in motion. First and foremost let me say that a soul can never be destroyed. The human body, or in the case of abortion, the human foetus, is just a vehicle in which to carry the soul, the spirit of who we really are, whilst we go through life on earth for our spiritual development. A soul may feel sadness that a particular opportunity to come to earth is lost. However, the soul can gain a lot spiritually from the experience of abortion. Indeed this may even be all that the soul needs to experience at the time. As the time approaches for a soul to come to the earthly plane, it goes through a great deal of preparation, with the help of spiritual guidance, as we saw in the chapter on 'pre-existence'. Our souls are trained, briefed and prepared for the experiences we may face, and are aware of the highest ideals we can achieve. As the time for entry to the earthly plane draws near, the soul descends from higher planes, and draws closer to the prospective parents.

At this point I feel the need to point out that having read several books relating to this and similar subjects, that it is considered by some, that it is the divine spark of the soul entering that makes its physical body grow, from the moment of conception. Therefore abortion is wrong, in all circumstances, as this action will destroy the divine spark.

I say respectfully divine energy cannot be destroyed, I have also read that the love between a man and woman during sexual intercourse is what draws the soul down into the mother's physical body, via a vortex of energy created during the sexual act. This is a very romantic notion. Of course love is a very powerful force that would encourage anyone closer, but what happens if someone is raped, and there is no love present? How does a soul descend then? The truth is that we exist in a world governed by the law of cause and effect. When sex takes place naturally, or via a test tube, 'the cause' – reproduction takes place, conception – 'the effect' occurs. Providing no other factor prevents it, the natural and biological laws have come into play. Of course the divine spark is present. The divine spark however is not the incoming soul. The soul has already been created of divine creative energy or God. The divine spark is just another word for divine creative energy or God by which all creation exists.

Therefore to sum up the divine spark, or if you prefer, divine creative energy, is triggered into action by the act of sexual intercourse, whether beautifully or badly expressed. This is the cause. Natural law ensues to manifest the effect, which is the beginning of the process of the biological creation of the physical body. Created from the divine creative energy, that creates all things: tables, chairs, computers, cells, everything. The physical can be destroyed, but the divine creative energy or God cannot. It is merely transmuted back to its original state, in this case, from foetus back to divine creative energy (see Chapter Two). The incoming soul is not transmuted back to divine creative energy however, just the physical body, which is temporary. The soul is permanent, and was created separately, from a different part of the divine creative energy, or more precisely God, at the beginning of creation.

When God gave us free will, he gave us the ability to co-create. In other words he allows us to use his energy. Just as a soul leaves a dead body, to return to spirit, so too does the soul return to spirit, if a foetus is destroyed, through abortion, or miscarriage. Therefore, only the physical is transmuted back to divine creative energy, subject to the natural laws of the decaying process. Or, if cremation is the process used, then the process is somewhat speeded up.

The incoming soul who has been standing by, to enter the newly created physical body, can in fact enter the body at any stage during the pregnancy. For instance, some souls, will choose to enter the physical at the moment of conception. Others will not enter until the moment of birth. Mostly the soul will come and go, spending some time with the physical, and the rest of the time, in spirit, taking final instruction. Each soul will spend time there according to their personal need for experience of the womb. Therefore at the time of abortion, the soul may not have entered the foetus but merely be standing by. Of course it would be impossible to actually know. From the soul's point of view, the degree to which disappointment is felt is dependent on how much that soul had integrated with the physical body. That is to say that, if a soul had not yet entered the physical properly, then awareness would be instantly remembered. But because the soul was still completely in contact with the spirit world, and therefore had a better understanding and perspective, compassion and respect for the prospective mother and her choice would accompany disappointment. Also there is the knowledge that a new arrangement can be made, either with someone else or that same person, in due course.

If on the other hand the soul had integrated with the physical completely, then a different situation arises. If a soul returns early from an incarnation; for example through abortion, cot death, or the death of a child from tragic circumstances, then the soul returns to spirit as the baby, small child, or foetus. For ages I wondered why it was that many mediums tell grieving parents that their child is growing up in spirit. They are not just saying this to comfort the parents and loved ones; it's really what they are getting through psychically. Auntie Maude is really looking after their little one. So why is it that a fully-grown soul can enter the womb, and then return to spirit as a helpless baby? I asked Heaven to explain to me. When the answer came to me it seemed so obvious; I don't know why I didn't realise it before. The moment the soul enters the physical body it starts to identify completely with its new surroundings. The vibrations become slower and denser, this creates a temporary amnesia concerning spiritual life, and the soul now focuses on earth life. So by the time the soul returns to spirit, it has so completely identified with the body of the baby. Before the soul can recover memory it has to continue on through the growing-up phase, as if on earth. Only now will the foetus, baby or little child be taken into loving care and brought up in the spirit world. If an Auntie Maude isn't able, there will be many willing and loving souls capable of giving the right care and attention, until the soul has grown enough to start recovering past memories of who they really are, and what happened and why. This process may be short or long, and is unique to the individual, as time does not exist in the spirit world. There is just a process of expanding consciousness, through knowledge and wisdom gained. However, soul memory will gradually re-emerge. The knowledge of the earth life just ended, albeit brief, is added to and enhances the beauty and wisdom of the soul, as does the experience and knowledge gained by the spirit child as he or she grows. Therefore the ongoing growing process of the child in spirit, is as important to the soul, as a child growing to adulthood on earth. All experience, good or bad is important. No soul ever misses out on a needed opportunity to grow spiritually. God the infinite intelligence has taken every eventuality into consideration. New arrangements are made constantly, because of our right to free will. A soul has many other things to learn whilst waiting to be born on earth, and when that time comes, may even be reunited with you. The divine plan is flexible.

I hope that from this you can see that abortion isn't wicked. It's just a choice. And because of God's eternal love we have the right to choose.

Chapter Seven

SPIRITUAL GUIDES

I CAN REMEMBER BEING QUITE IMPRESSED WHEN A MEDIUM, whom I had been to visit, told me that I had a North American Indian chief as my spiritual guide, or spirit guide as she called him. She told me that my guide was a bit cross with me, because I hadn't been listening to him, but that I would do from now on. (I didn't know that this was a big give-away. That he was an imposter. But then I didn't know all that I know now). So I listened to what the medium told me with awe and respect. She was very sincere and told me a lot of things that were correct, but information about my spiritual guide was not one of them. However I became very fond and enamoured with 'Running Deer', which was apparently his name. I was also rather impressed that I had a big chief at that. It pleased me to think he was following me everywhere (another misconception), guiding me and helping me. I suddenly found in my visualisations and meditations that he'd turn up, he'd always be there with me, because I wanted him to be there. But he never said anything, never made any profound statements, or told me anything about my future, my spiritual progress, or what might be expected of me. Whereas other people I knew who were 'in touch' with their spirit guides, had amazing revelations, and were told all sorts of wonderful things. So why didn't I have a guide like that? I began to get a bit disenchanted, and wondered if my guide thought I didn't believe in him enough. But I did! Or at least I did believe I had a spiritual guide, I always did believe that; long before I went to see the medium.

Anyway I found myself sitting on my bed one day, praying, talking, I thought, to Running Deer, explaining that I did believe in spiritual guides, I did believe he was there.

'I know you are there,' I said. 'I know you are there, I can feel you. I've even heard you in the past,' (referring to the incident in the car, when I was told 'don't go with him') 'I know you are there!'

Well this went on for ages with me wittering on, my eyes closed, and being very sincere. Then something truly amazing happened, something that was to gradually change my understanding completely. It only lasted for a few seconds, but it shut me up, and stopped me in my tracks. There, suddenly, in my mind's eye, I saw a blinding white light and seven people standing in a semi-circle, smiling at me. Some were male and some female. I couldn't say for sure how many of each, but I think two were women, the rest men. I remembered that one man had dark hair and a beard, one woman had short dark curly hair, the other long blonde hair. I cannot remember them all, everything happened so quickly. I couldn't see their faces clearly because the light was so bright and they were all shining. They all wore long white robes. They just stood quietly smiling lovingly at me and the love that emanated from them was truly amazing. After watching them slowly fade out of sight, I just knelt on the bed, stunned and speechless, unable to move, not daring to open my eyes, in case they came back, and I missed them. After what seemed like forever, I opened my eyes, and slowly gathered myself together.

I often joke that the reason they showed themselves to me was so they could get some peace. But, joking aside, I believe there were two main reasons for their letting me see them. One because I believed so much that I was being guided, and secondly so that I should not be misguided into believing in a thought form image, which is what Running Deer turned out to be. Later on I realised how important that understanding would be.

I also realised that we don't necessarily only have one spiritual guide each, as I appeared to have seven. Perhaps I'm a particularly awkward customer, I thought, difficult to handle, nothing would surprise me! Eventually over a period of time, once I had got over my shock and surprise, and it had started to sink in naturally, I gave the subject much thought and prayed for a true understanding, not only for myself, but that I might share with others who may be being similarly misled. By now I recognised Running Deer for what he was. Just a thought form, planted, not maliciously, I might add, by the medium, and encouraged to grow

71

by me, and who I, albeit unconsciously, put into my own meditations. He was rather like a cartoon character; animated, but no real life, no spirit, no love, no real feelings, and certainly no real wisdom. In fact, everything I had seen in my true spiritual guides, he was not. And so he died a death, in just a few months after his birth, which was most fortunate for me. A valuable lesson, but for others not so fortunate, as they can easily be misled by thought forms and imposter spirits, for whole lifetimes.

Now, before anyone leaps to the defence of their spiritual guide, not all North American Indians, monks, nuns, etcetera, are imposters, I didn't say that. So how can you tell if your spiritual guide is a true spiritual guide? It was a question I put to God, and my spiritual guides, along with several other questions, I hoped would be answered for me, and I wasn't disappointed.

One evening whilst reading a book quietly as my husband sat at the table marking another batch of books (he was a teacher), I could hear a voice speaking to me. I was told to just sit quietly and listen. I thought about getting a paper and pen, but was told, 'Don't worry now, just listen. You will have time to write it all down afterwards. You won't forget what you have been told.'

So I listened quietly, whilst I was told all about spiritual guides. After this I wrote it all down in rough, and now here is the tidy version of what I was told.

True spiritual guides are highly evolved souls who have no more need to return to earth, as they have learned as much as they need to learn, from the earth plane, and are therefore qualified to give guidance. Before a spiritual guide can become just that they undergo the necessary training, as it is not enough to have had experience of earth life. Each spiritual guide is assigned to work as part of a team with other spiritual guides who, likewise, have been assigned, in agreement with the soul of the individual whom they will be guiding. Each team member has been specifically chosen for the skills and experiences they themselves have and that can be of value to the incarnating soul whilst on the earth. Since every incarnate soul has different lessons to learn and needs different skills and experiences, the number of spiritual guides they will have will differ from person to person.

Each spiritual guide in the team may work with the person

individually as well as part of the team. For instance a person may need special guidance during special training for a particular job. Therefore a guide on the team with appropriate understanding would become more prominent during the training period of the person's life. However, because each individual has a God-given right to free will, the person may reject time after time the opportunity to follow the path that would give them the chance to train for a specific job. In that case, the spiritual guide, chosen for their skill to help in this particular matter, may find that their need to step forward, so to speak, postponed for a while, and indeed sometimes they may never have the opportunity to help in their specialist field during a whole lifetime. In this event the spiritual guide will just continue to help out as a member of the team. However it is safe to say that for each guide, the work they will have to undertake during the individual's lifetime, is much and varied. They will have their work cut out. It will be a far more complex situation than the very simple example that I have given here.

Although each spiritual guide is a highly evolved soul, they too have room to evolve further, and therefore can gain a great deal spiritually by taking on such a noble mission. Your spiritual guides are contracted to you for your entire lifetime. As one may move more to the forefront and another seems to step back, it could give the impression that your guide has changed. In reality they are all part of a team, that is constantly working as one, throughout your entire lifetime.

Our true spiritual guides are appointed to us by their higher masters, and ultimately by God. True spiritual guides are never self-appointed. To help you recognise a true spiritual guide, you need to recognise that first and foremost, they love you unconditionally. This means that they treat you with respect, they always honour your right to free will, they are firm, fair, kind and consistent. They don't sulk, they don't chastise, they don't get angry, and they don't blame. They never leave you all alone, without help. Neither incidentally do they travel around behind you on every bus, or sit outside the bedroom whilst you are having sexual relations. They have a life of their own. They do not intrude into yours. Since they are in a state of pure consciousness, they are multidimensional, which means, they can be in more than one place at a time. They have no need to follow you around in order to help you.

If you are lucky enough to be clairvoyant or clairaudient, you can see or hear your spiritual guides on a regular basis. Don't expect them to stand on a pedestal full of self-importance. They won't ever order you to do anything, or tell you what to do. Neither will they boast to you about their personal achievements or their hardships during their life on earth. They don't need to prove themselves.

In other words, the highly evolved souls that spiritual guides are do not display the kind of human failings and vanities that we ourselves have. If your spiritual guides are temperamental in any way, you should be questioning their validity.

What do spiritual guides look like? In truth, they are pure consciousness, balls of shining light (as are we all); who project a physical appearance, as this is aesthetically pleasing. Most people in the astral planes, after being there for a while, choose to wear the beautiful robes like the ones I saw my spiritual guides wearing. In actual fact these robes are not so much a material, but more a projection of light. Although lots appear to be white, I believe that there are many shades of colour. However it isn't compulsory to wear robes. A guide might therefore wear whatever they felt would be most acceptable to the soul individual that they were looking after. This then may be the clothing that they may have worn in their last incarnation on earth, or perhaps even modern clothing. On the other hand, if an individual had a belief that meant they expected to have a North American Indian, Tibetan monk etcetera, as a spiritual guide, then he, the individual would project his own beliefs on to his spiritual guides. In other words, the individual would see or feel whatever he expected to see or feel. He would create personality, name, nationality etcetera for his guide, out of his own thoughts, create thought forms, to clothe and disguise his guide to match his beliefs and expectation. This is mostly harmless and done quite unconsciously on the part of the individual, and a true spiritual guide won't try to force a change. The individual will do that himself as he evolves. Clothing and names are of little importance to a spiritual guide, but they seem to matter more to us. It is possible that every member of the team of spiritual guides, whether male or female, will be known to the individual for a whole lifetime, as his beloved Indian or Chinese monk, even though the style of guidance may change for a while, as one member of the team moves forward and another back, and therefore the energy would be different. From the individual's point of view, he just sees the beloved guide as behaving a bit differently lately, while some people will recognise the energy change, and invent, albeit unconsciously, a new character to fit the new energy. True spiritual guides are so infused with light that it is difficult to really see them properly, as I found out. Therefore many who are mediumistic, clairvoyant or who meditate regularly create images from the thoughts and feelings that emanate from their guides, but this doesn't mean that they are not in touch with true guidance.

Likewise some people who tune into their higher self, the soul self, will characterise what they feel. In itself this isn't a bad thing, but inevitably can cause confusion. Together with a vivid imagination, an individual can create many guiding spirits from thought forms. Although thought forms themselves are pretty harmless, they can become dangerous to the individual, when the individual starts to interact with the thought forms, and the thought form guides start giving advice and guidance that the individual acts upon, because in effect the individual is guiding himself, usually from an imperfect human point of view, and not a higher wisdom point of view. (This isn't the same as symbolic meditational work, where we learn to understand ourselves better).

More disturbing than this are imposter spirits. If true spiritual guidance is not being heard, then the individual becomes very vulnerable to the intrusion of imposter spirits. These spirits are beings who live on the lower astral planes. They have not evolved enough to be a true spiritual guide, but for reasons best known to themselves, they fancy themselves in the role of spiritual guide. They hone in on the individual's thought forms, which by now are pretty well established (the more energy you give to a thought, the stronger it becomes). These so-called guides are on a power trip or perhaps they have chips on their shoulders, because they failed in someway. They may want to lead you up the garden path, and away from true guidance. To be fair, some may be sincere, but misguided, but they will all prevent you from following your true spiritual guidance, and therefore the fulfilment of your true spiritual mission. They are, in fact, quite easy to recognise, as they will flatter both you and themselves.

They may show you many fantastic things, psychic in nature, impress you, drain your energy, feed off you, lead you into trouble or sensationalism, all disguised as 'spiritual truth'. They can be very clever. It's so easy to get swept along with the tide. Instead of being in touch with the truth, you very quickly become further from it than when you started.

Imposter guides are most likely to be encountered during meditation where proper guidance and tuition in the art have not been sought.

Imposter guides are likely to be no more advanced spiritually than the highest level of consciousness that you yourself are operating on, during your meditation. It is important to understand the traps and pitfalls that you may encounter whilst meditating.

Often, as was the case, I believe, with myself. A medium may tell you that you have, for example, a North American Indian chief as a spirit guide. When in fact what the medium may have tuned into is an aspect of your personality. For example, the strong willed part of your nature, which the medium interprets as a strong character then adds albeit innocently the colouring of her own beliefs about guides. Giving the resulting impression of a North American Indian chief. If a quieter aspect of your nature is tapped into then a nun for example may be the resulting characterisation. This then may become the thought form that you unsuspectingly use to guide yourself during meditation. Or more dangerously attract an imposter spirit, who will then use the thought form character to operate through.

Of course, there are kindly souls such as relatives and friends who just want to help. Whilst some may indeed be very advanced souls, and very aware, not all necessarily know or understand the individual's spiritual goal or needs. Therefore this kind of guidance, whilst kindly meant, can still be detrimental to spiritual progress. The individual should not allow himself to become too dependent on guidance from a deceased loved one. Loved ones will always want to help and comfort, and will often give their opinions about our lives, our relationships, and lose no time in coming through a psychic channel, known as a medium, if they can orchestrate a way of getting you to see one, in order to give opinions and advice.

When we love someone who has died, we want to be comforted by them; we want to be guided by them. It's only natural. But just because they have died doesn't mean that they are suddenly all worldly wise, impartial, and non-judgmental. Therefore this kind of guidance should be considered very carefully. So don't be afraid to question the wisdom of their guidance. After all, you didn't do everything Aunt Evelyn suggested when she was alive, so what has changed?

Our true spiritual guides work very hard to try and protect us, and lead us in the right direction. However, chatter in our minds, beliefs, ego, stubbornness and other things create confusion. It is very easy to be drawn in by psychic glamour, or to convince yourself that you should take action that makes you feel better; to hear what you want to hear, or do what you have always done, because you feel comfortable, to take the easy way out. If you think you hear a voice telling you to take revenge on someone, because they hurt you, forget it. It's false guidance, probably you speaking to yourself. Neither God, nor true spiritual guidance, will tell you to do anything that is other than for the highest good for all concerned. If things don't seem too clear, keep focusing on doing the right thing, and keep asking to be shown what that is. Ask for help, be quiet, humble yourself a little, open your heart and mind and drop preconceived ideas. Stop defending your injured pride. Just listen and wait, you will be truly guided. Guidance comes in different and varied ways, and not always straight away. It will be different for each person, but once it arrives it is always recognisable by the feeling of great peace that accompanies it. Higher wisdom comes through you. Don't forget you are an integral part of the team!

Angels

I thought that before I closed this chapter I would leave you with an interesting thought about angels, those glorious heavenly bodies, depicted with long robes, halos, trumpets and harps, flying though the clouds and heavens with enormous white wings. Since biblical times, angels have been depicted in this way. For hundreds of years artists have painted angels floating around with giant wings that seem to start from above the head and reaching their feet, with shining halos above the head. This image has been passed down for centuries, from generation to generation, and has never really changed and never really questioned in great depth. So do angels really have wings? I don't believe they do. Already I can hear traditionalists protesting, but it says quite clearly in the Bible, white robes, halos, trumpets and wings. I've been brought up with the same understanding. I'm sure that the people who first saw the archangels and angels in biblical times really gave a sincere and as accurate description of what they saw and understood at the time. I'm not trying to dispute that, but what did they actually see?

I believe that angels don't actually need wings, in order to get around. What is the point when in the spirit world, travel is possible by thought process? We think where we want to be and in an instant we are there. Also I believe that angels in their truest form are shining balls of light energy, just as are all spiritual entities whether angelic or human souls, (the Bible also refers to angels as wheels of fire). However angels (as also human souls in spirit) have the ability to appear in human form, usually for our sakes. After all, angels are messengers (angel means messenger).

Communication is probably helped if we humans can identify with the messenger. White robes seem to be traditional dress in the spirit world, although human souls on arrival back in the spirit world after physical death, can wear whatever they please, for as long as it pleases them. In the same way, although traditionally angels are seen in white robes, they can also manifest themselves in everyday modern clothing, if they think that you will feel more comfortable with that image. If you fervently believe that angels have wings they may appear with wings; it doesn't matter to them, so long as they achieve the aim that they have come for.

So what about wings and halos? Well, as I said, I don't think angels really have wings, but what I do believe that people who have seen angels do see, is the auric energy field that surrounds them and all living things. We all have an energy field or an aura as it is known, surrounding the physical body. In fact, the aura isn't just around us; it goes through us and emanates from us. Essentially the auric energy field is us, the real us, the part of us that goes to the spirit world after the death of our physical bodies. This energy field contains our souls. Just as all living things have energy fields or auras, so do angels. After all, they are living, even though they never incarnate on earth. They can take on human physical form, if the mission they are carrying out requires it. Just as angels do not experience human life and death, neither do humans become angels; we may become messengers, but not angels, who are pure. Our path lies in a different direction. So, angels as living energy in their purest state, are like balls of pure conscious light, or wheels of fire! When they manifest themselves as humans they become auric energy fields surrounding and shining through the physical projection. Because angels are pure they come from the highest spiritual realms. The higher the realm, the faster the vibrational rate (the physical body vibrates at a very slow rate, hence our density and ability to appear solid). Therefore when a human being sees an angel, what they see is a very pure white or golden light, surrounding what looks like a person in a white gown, and a fast moving vibratory rate which appears to flutter and gives the appearance of feathers because of the shape of the auric energy field, which is egg shaped. It is easy to interpret this phenomena as a pair of giant wings, that extend above and below the body of the angel, especially if you have little understanding of such things as energy fields, molecules, atoms, and vibrations. This was probably the case in Biblical times.

The halo is also part of the auric energy field. In actual fact it is more like a crescent or wide U-shape that sits some eight inches above the crown of the head. In all of our energy fields there are energy vortexes known as chakras. The main ones known to us are: the base, the sacral, solar plexus, heart, throat, pituitary gland and the crown. (There are many good books that explain the aura and chakra system in greater detail.) The halo therefore is in fact the spiritual vortex known as the crown chakra. All human souls have one. Not just saints and angels as depicted in paintings. It's just that the more spiritually evolved a soul is, the brighter it will appear to those who have clear sight (clairvoyance). Hence the reason why painters have been inspired to paint angels with halos in the shape of circles or semi-circles around the head.

In conclusion I would like to share a personal experience, that

I myself have had. As a spiritual healer, I often perform distance healing; that is to say, I channel healing energy to a person, who cannot be present, by holding them in my mind's eye. My experience occurred in the early days of my healing experience. I didn't know much about the auric energy field or vibratory rates. I was still in my probationary period, and had much still to learn. Anyway I settled down to send distance healing to a friend who was troubled. I do this by channelling divine healing energy, but I was also sending my own thoughts of love and compassion. I could see my friend, in my mind's eye, from a distance, standing in light. As I reached out from my heart with love to my friend, I became aware of myself enveloping him in light, as if I had reached out with my arms. Yet my arms, in my mind's eye, and in reality, were by my side. In fact it was my energy field that was wrapping around him. I could see this energy field expanding. It also seemed to be fluttering, and was feather-like in appearance. To all intents and purpose it looked like I had wrapped wings around him. I was very aware that I felt unconditional love and compassion, and yet another part of me, that was watching what I was doing, was in complete awe of what I was experiencing.

(Even after all these years as a healer, I am still in awe of what I see and experience.) I had no idea of what we are capable of doing. Was it just my imagination? Of course I cannot prove it, but I can say I did not have this knowledge before my experience. However I prefer to believe that, as we raise our consciousness on to a higher level, as when sending thoughts of unconditional love, we are in tune with our soul selves and our auric energy field vibrates at a faster rate. What I thought I saw was my higher consciousness reaching out to my friend, as my thoughts of love and compassion, embraced him. After all what else could it be? I'm no angel, and I definitely haven't got wings!

Chapter Eight
REINCARNATION

I F THE CHAPTER ON THE PRE-EXISTENCE AND PREDESTINATION was like a disjointed rose, then this chapter could be described as describing the colour pink to someone who has never seen pink – very difficult. So I will endeavour to give it my best shot. In this chapter I won't discuss karma, which goes hand in hand with the subject of reincarnation, I thought we'd cover that in Part Two.

The traditional view of reincarnation is, in a nutshell, that when a person dies, they go to Heaven, review the life they have just lived, plan a new life, then come back to earth to have another go, to see if they can improve, get things right, sort out wrongs, old hurts, unfinished business. I don't have a problem with this. It's just that being myself, I question things a lot. It seemed to me that there must be more to it than that. Something about reincarnation wasn't right. So I prayed for guidance.

'Do we reincarnate or not?' I asked.

Yes and no, was the answer I received.

Of course I was confused, and of course I asked many more questions. Since then I have been on a very long metaphorical journey. I'm afraid to say I haven't got all of the answers yet; perhaps I never will. However I have decided to write down what I have found out about this vast subject.

In the spirit world the past, present and future all exist simultaneously. That is to say, past memories (Akashic records) exist in the ether, alongside the future potential that is constantly being created by our thoughts, feelings and beliefs, which also are held in the ether. In the spirit world, just as in the physical world, we are mostly living within the present moment, our consciousness occupied by what we are doing at that moment in time. In the physical state a trip into our past is just a memory, a daydream. However in the spirit world we can actually go back in time. By thinking of a specific moment in past time, we are transported back to that time. We can interact and immerse within that time either completely either by reliving the experience in its entirety, or we can observe the experience as if watching a movie. We can interact similarly within our potential future. Incidentally you don't have to be resident in the spirit world to do this. You can do this whilst incarnate on the earth, during sleep state or hypnosis, as we all visit the spirit world whilst we sleep. This is our natural state. But of course upon waking, your experience, should you remember it, will have a dream like quality. The intensity of the experience is somewhat masked by the physical body.

Linear time does not exist within the spirit world. This is why the earth, which vibrates at a slower rate, creating a heavier and more solid world, is the best place to go for our education and experiences, as linear time becomes possible. Linear time is needed in order to maintain balance, that is to say that if it were possible to live our incarnations on earth out of time sequence, the effects would be utter chaos, as we would constantly be changing things, as an action taken one moment in time will affect what happens in the future and in this case if it were possible, vice versa. The law of cause and effect is not subject to a time frame. It just is, and just as on earth, the spirit world has its laws as well, that is to say it is governed by the natural laws of the universe.

By slowing the vibrations down, time can be created. If you were able to speed time up to the same vibration as the spirit world, you would find that everything would be happening at once, as it does in the spirit world. Therefore, whilst it appears to us that reincarnation takes place, from a spirit world perspective, it doesn't really happen at all, even though we do have several lives that we live on earth.

Since my knowledge of quantum physics is probably less than half a postage stamp, let's pretend that the spirit world operates on a similar system to us on earth, and look at how reincarnation takes place.

The Plan

It is already known that we will need much experience in order to achieve and accomplish our spiritual goal. Therefore our personal plan is worked out in advance, and that includes the many lives that we will need to experience on the earth plane, as well as the experiences we will need in the many other spheres of existence. (I don't know what or where these spheres are, I just know that this isn't all that there is). Our lives are not chosen in advance because of the mess we have made in the last one. We will get to that bit later. Firstly and foremost our lives are designed as an education and training ground for the spiritual purpose that each soul, as an individual, has chosen to fulfil as their part within the higher and larger plan. Along with our education, provision is made and understood as an essential and integral part for the working out of mistakes. On earth these periods in our life are known to many as karmic periods. These karmic periods are the parts of our lives most associated with reincarnation, making reincarnation seem rather melodramatic and fatalistic, with much emphasis placed on the bad that must have been entered into in a 'past life'!

From the spirit world point of view, our lives are experienced simultaneously, as we are multidimensional souls. However, even in the spirit world, a spirit of average evolutionary development would only be aware of the life to which they were currently giving their attention to, since we do not become instantly all-knowing at the moment of death, or, if you like, re-entry into the spirit world. Your awareness would only be with you and your current beliefs and understanding, until you explored and realised more of the truth. In other words you would not necessarily be aware of other dimensions or levels of consciousness.

From a more linear and therefore earthly point of view our lives have been set up like an ongoing chain of events to which we move our consciousness from one part of the chain to another, pausing in between each life in order to assimilate the lessons we have learned, to review our progress and access any further needs we may have; not to mention to have a well-earned rest before we move on and enter the earth environment once again.

So far this process all seems pretty easy, but because of inexperience and free will, we are bound to make many mistakes, do things we later regret, or not do things we wish we had and so on. Even a silly mistake or negligent action that results in losing one's life before one was meant to, and before one had completed the lessons one should have had. So called accidents are not incidentally random events, but a culmination of thought processes, actions, decisions and choices, either made consciously or subconsciously, which attract us toward an accident situation.

So our past actions have to be catered for within our personal evolutionary plan and this is very flexible. Therefore additional arrangements are added which at the appropriate time on earth will be activated by events that allow an evolvement to a better conclusion than that which was less satisfactory in the past.

Because of our need for experience, we do not necessarily try to put right our mistakes, or keep trying a particular lesson straight away in the very next life in the chain. We may have to wait until we have gained more experience. We may also have to wait for others, whom we need to work with, to be available to work with again. So we may not come across the same life experience with the same person for several lifetimes down the line. In earth time this may be several hundreds of years. The issues that need healing do not leave us, but lie dormant, until activated by appropriate stimuli. Our lifetimes may also include more karmic work in one lifetime, and not so much in another. Dealing with a lot in one lifetime doesn't make you a really bad person in the past, or a better person just because you don't appear to have a lot to do. We cover whatever is appropriate within the conditions that we have at the time, and of course we may need to learn more, before we can hope to achieve a better result. (You wouldn't expect an apprentice carpenter to make a complicated piece of furniture without knowledge and experience.)

In the meantime we give our consciousness to the next life in the chain, as there is a lot to learn, and much to do.

As we make our way through this succession of lives, correcting and refining, our consciousness is expanding, our soul is evolving. Incidentally, if a life is cut short on earth, the process of growing up and maturing continues in the spirit world, whilst learning as much as can be learned without earth conditions, as the continuity of the personality is essential.

The personality of the soul does not change, as reincarnation may suggest. As we enter a new physical body, we do not mask an old personality with a new one; we do not have hundreds of personalities that get all mixed up together as if they were a stew. You are not lost when the soul inhabits a new physical body, as though the soul had discarded you in favour of the new personality, leaving you as an empty shell, wandering until you disappear back into the collective consciousness.

You are the soul, your soul is you, your personality is part of you, your soul. What is really happening is that, as you progress onward, you, your personality is growing, refining and enriching, your consciousness is expanding, and you, your soul is evolving, through experience. You are gradually becoming your higher self, expressed through the physical. The soul reflects our wisdom and therefore our inner beauty. Our higher self is the outward expression of that wisdom and beauty. When our spirit indulges in the negative, our higher self becomes masked by a lower self, as can be seen in the lower astral planes, where the outward expression becomes one of ugliness and distortion.

This is why in the higher astral planes and beyond a soul looks beautiful, and in the lower realms they look ugly, dirty or pitiful.

Age in the Spirit World

Many religions teach that a soul takes on their optimum age, i.e. around about the age of thirty, when in the spirit realms. To an extent this is true, as all signs of age, such as wrinkles, grey hair, baldness, painful crooked limbs all disappear, unless you like a bit of grey, or baldness. You can project your preferred image! Generally what is left, is the inner beauty and wisdom of the soul. However as a soul grows in wisdom, and evolves, so too does the outer expression; that is to say, that the soul is essentially the same in appearance, but grows more mature, more developed, minus the wrinkles of course. The wisdom and therefore the love that emanates from these souls, is such that to the onlooker, especially from an earthbound point of view, where time is part of our understanding, we would naturally interpret that wisdom as age, and yet, there is an unmistakable inner beauty and glory.

For instance, when I saw my spiritual guides, they were shining, beautiful, and radiant in a golden white light; so bright, it was difficult to see them very clearly. It happened in only about two, maybe, three seconds, in actual time.

The love that emanated from them was incredible. I was rendered speechless. They looked agelessly beautiful, yet mature. If you asked me to put an age on them, I would have to say it was nearer fifty than thirty. They seemed like ordinary everyday sort of people and yet there was nothing ordinary about them at all. I have never seen such beauty, felt such love or encountered such wisdom, save for the Lord Jesus himself. I am quite sure that my encounter with Christ consciousness was toned down quite considerably, because I don't honestly think I would be able to cope with the level of wisdom and beauty that emanates from the beautiful soul that is our Lord Jesus.

Genetic and Cellular Memories

All living things have an aura, or auric energy field. This also includes living cells. We are made up of millions of cells, and we have an energy field that not only surrounds us, but is also through us, within us, is us. This energy field contains all of our thoughts and feelings and memories, both positive and negative. If our thoughts and feelings are strong enough they will create the reality that we live in the physical world. In this way the cells in our body are affected by our thoughts and feelings, as whatever stays in the energy field for long enough, will eventually manifest within the physical, given enough time. For instance constant thoughts of bitterness or resentment could eventually manifest as negative energy within the cells of the body, which in turn create disease. Our cells are constantly regenerating. I believe in the space of about seven years, or something like that, the entire physical body is remade. Of course it is an ongoing process and therefore a very subtle process. If an old hurt, fear or bad attitude is not healed, let go of or forgiven, then the new cell soon becomes similarly impregnated with the same negative memory energy, via the energy field. Our body becomes increasingly vulnerable to disease and ill health. If, on the other hand, a positive action on our part takes place, such as healing old hurts, forgiving, letting go, overcoming fear, then the new cell that comes to take over from the old dead cell will not be subject to the old negative memory, but new healing memory instead. In this way a potential disease has been averted, for now at least. Because of life experiences being what they are, it means that new cells can still fall prey to any new negative thoughts and actions that we may indulge in.

It isn't too difficult to see how cellular memories are passed from mother to baby during pregnancy, when not only is the baby growing within the mother's auric energy field, but is created from the cells of both mother and father. To take a step further, our ancestors' memories can similarly be passed from generation to generation, just as inherited diseases, eye and hair colour, mannerisms are passed down genetically. Jung identified the former as the collective unconscious.

When we choose our parents we know in advance the kind of issues, beliefs and prejudice to which we will be subjected. If we have old hurts and issues from a previous life that need healing and, because like attracts like, we will attract from our parents, either from their cells during pregnancy, or from day to day interaction with them, what we need to act as a trigger or stimuli, to encourage us to take appropriate action toward our own healing process. We are not exactly taking on the 'sins of our fathers' or if you prefer their past karma, we just attract from them a reflection of that which remains unresolved within us. If you don't need something from your parents, then you will not attract it, even though you may be surrounded by it. But whether you attract a potential disease, a bad attitude or perhaps you seem to be repeating history, just as your mother or grandmother did before you, you have attracted it so that you can do something about it. If you find healing solutions to some of these problems, perhaps you will have opportunity to help your parents, maybe just by example, because we are all pupil and teacher to each other.

Akashic Records

Because energy cannot be destroyed, everything that we experience and all of our memories are recorded in the ether. Many philosophies refer to this phenomenon as the Akashic records, a place where all of our memories and experiences are recorded in a large book. I suppose in western society, we would refer to the book that St Peter is holding when we enter the pearly gates. Since many things in the astral planes of existence are a matter of perception, the book could appear to you as a computer, that you could tap into and access information. How you perceive the Akashic records isn't important. The fact is that everything is recorded in the ether, and we have access to the information stored there. That is to say you have limited access, according to your personal level of spiritual development and need to know. In the Akashic records are your personal experiences, past and present, along with experiences of all others who have ever been on the earth plane.

In the spirit world it is possible to access the memories of other souls, and experience their experiences. This is a good way of learning from others, and perhaps arm yourself with extra experience and knowledge, before you enter the earth plane for your own earth experience. Because you have no physical body in the spirit world, it is very easy to integrate another soul's memories and completely identify them as your own. It's a bit like getting completely absorbed in a novel that you can't put down. You identify with the hero; your heart races as he works his way out of a sticky situation. You feel like crying as his heart breaks for a lost love.

If a soul completely identifies with a past experience of another soul, it is easy for them to believe that they themselves have had this particular experience. It is also possible to access the Akashic records, albeit in a limited way whilst we are on the earth, during dream state, meditation and hypnotherapy to name the most common ways. This is one of our sources of inspiration and ideas. In actual fact, we are walking among the ether all of the time, but we are most likely to access it when we are quiet and relaxed. Sometimes when I am in that semi-conscious state, just before sleep, I can hear lots of chatter. It's a bit like being between two positions on a radio; you cannot hear very clearly what is being said, until you tune into the right frequency.

Hypnotherapy has been used as a major tool in trying to access past life memories, and used as evidence to try and prove reincarnation. Whilst I do believe we live more than one physical life, I do not believe that we experience as many lives as a lot of people would have us believe. I have read and heard of many stories of people who claim to have regressed through hypnotherapy many times, and each time they have discovered a different past life, for them. The experience has been completely authentic. Now, I'm not going to say, I don't think it's true, or that it is impossible. A good hypnotherapist can usually tell if someone is just having experiences based on a wonderful imagination or not. However I firmly believe that when a person is nicely relaxed, with the help of the hypnotherapist, and asked to go back in time to 'a past life', and this is the key – into *a* past life, this isn't the same as 'one of your own past lives, if you have had any', (the subconscious mind obeys a command literally). They then do access a past life, from the Akashic records.

In some cases the person may access a famous life, in order to satisfy an unconscious need to increase their level of self-esteem or fulfil some other need within them. Then there will be those who are looking for a solution to a personal problem, by accessing a past life that is similar to their own present experience. It is possible to effect a genuine healing of a problem in their own life, so it is a good and useful therapy. Since like attracts like, it is very easy to access a past life experience that quite parallels your own experience in many aspects. I believe that this could explain at least one reason why so many people claim to be the one and only Cleopatra, or Napoleon. Of course many people have experience of many ordinary everyday types, but this does not necessarily mean that this is better proof that the past life experience was of one of the subject's own past lives. Then there is the question of the authenticity of the experience, as some people, who are hypnotised, only lightly experience the past life, while others will experience intensity of emotion and even pain.

So does it mean that the light experience is not authentic,

whilst the intense experience is? Well to both I'd say yes and no. Just as it is possible to completely identify with another soul's experience in the spirit world, so it is possible to have a similar experience under hypnosis. Therefore the experience that you report back to the hypnotherapist can be an intense or peripheral one, of either your own or someone else's past life. I think this ability to access the Akashic records may also give the reason why many people seem to chop and change gender from one incarnation to another with such frequency. I should think that it is virtually impossible to find out which experiences are a person's true past life experiences, as most of the experiences are valid, in that they are true past lives, but not necessarily the subject's own.

I cannot be certain, but I do not believe that we change sex during our incarnations on earth, as I believe that we have always existed and always will, that is to say that our soul carries a blueprint, a pattern if you like. I believe that blueprint has a tendency toward one sex, whilst the blueprint of our twin soul carries a tendency toward the opposite sex, even though we are all created by androgynous energy. Despite the many books and testimonies I have read from those who have experienced past life recall whilst under hypnosis, where they sincerely claim to have experienced memories of a life as a member of the opposite sex, I cannot conclude that this is sufficient evidence to prove to me that we change sex when we reincarnate. However, where past-life memories are concerned, it is possible to access any sex, as it is the memories and experiences that we are drawing to us, rather than the sex of the person whose life we may have drawn to us. Just as you can pick up and read a red book, you can also read a blue book. But with the physical body, I believe it has to have the right vibrations. A bit like your personal signature tune. As I have said, this is a personal belief, and I cannot conclude with certainty either way.

Incidentally it might be worth mentioning that because your body has your vibrations it is not possible for a desperate soul stuck on the lower astral planes, and wanting to quickly return to earth, to steal your body before you have time to take up your rightful place.

Sometimes, during hypnotherapy, it is possible for a desperate soul, who wants to be heard, to use your physical faculties, such as your voice, whilst you are in a relaxed state under hypnosis. But this can only be temporary because of different vibrations and your soul's will. (This is not the same as a spirit person becoming attached to you.) In such a case where this soul relates their story through you, it would not be difficult for you to believe afterwards that you had been in contact with one of your own past lives.

Recalibration

Let us assume that we are ready to take our next trip into the earth plane. We've done our homework, we know what we are going to be doing down there. We know what is expected of us. Our spiritual guides will be near by to help us, and our new mother and father are on earth waiting for us, so let's get going!

As you make your descent to the physical world, the energy becomes denser and heavier. You are attracting this energy to you all the time, and since like attracts like, you will attract to yourself what corresponds to the energy within your own energy field, starting with the mental planes, then the emotional planes, and finally the etheric plane. Because like attracts like, it is during the recalibration process that you attract both positive and negative energies to yourself. That is to say if you are carrying unhealed hurts, unfinished business, unkind attitudes within your energy field you will attract similar energy toward you. This also goes for the good bits about you.

Depending on the level of consciousness in which the hurt exists, be it mental or emotional, that will be the area that you will attract from. For example if you have an emotional hang-up, it will be during your descent through the emotional planes of existence that you will attract the corresponding energy. By the time you reach the etheric energy field, which is the energy field surrounding the earth, you might start to attract negative energy that will manifest deformity in the physical body, or possibly energy that may attract an accident in the future, unless, you effect some kind of healing, or correction. (Please remember that this description is in a very simplistic form.) On entry into the physical body, you accept the DNA, the genetic make-up and inherited medical history, along with the memories encoded into the cells of the body that was created for you during procreation, inherited from your new mother, father and both ancestral lines.

The moment of our birth is very important. In order that we might learn, grow and heal old hurts, we need a trigger to stimulate us into action; the stimulants will be transient conditions and influences that will affect us on all levels: mental, emotional, physical and spiritual. These transient conditions and influences help us to attract to ourselves the lessons that we need to learn, and may manifest themselves as a new job, moving house, or even someone tall, dark and handsome! These are examples of catalysts, but they all come with, shall we say, a gift. An opportunity to learn a much needed lesson, or to heal an old festering wound. But don't forget, you agreed to these things in advance. You agreed to meet tall dark and handsome, and he agreed to meet you. Now it gets complicated because of free will and the most famous aspect of reincarnation – 'karma'. Let's close this chapter now and I'll see you again on earth, in Part Two!

Chapter Nine

KARMA

KARMA SEEMS TO BE THE NEW BUZZWORD AT THE MOMENT. It slips into people's everyday conversation, like washing powder!

'What did I do to deserve all this aggravation? I know! It must have been something I did in a past life. This is just my karma, I must have been really awful!'

If you ask people to explain what karma is, those who know something about it will tell you it is related to reincarnation. It's part of the Buddhist religious belief, or perhaps part of the 'new age movement'. Some may tell you its God's wrath, for past misdeeds, or to do with the law of cause and effect. Some might say that those who are disabled are working out a lot of bad karma, or maybe someone may say, my husband and I are in a karmic relationship. That's why we have to stay together even though we are unhappy! Or if you are wicked in one life and harm someone, then you have to experience some harmful event in the next life, probably at the hands of the person who you harmed in the past life.

As you can see misinformation can escalate into a huge myth, and can be very dangerous and very disheartening to anyone who happens to be going through a rough patch in their life. It would be very soul-destroying and depressing to hear someone tell you, for instance, that the reason they thought you are in debt and in trouble with the courts and never seem to have any money was probably because you were greedy in a past life and took too much from a poor community and left them starving whilst you prospered. So now you have to know what it's like to go without!

It isn't any wonder that the subject of reincarnation gets such bad press. This may be why those who try to teach about karma and the law of cause and effect may get referred to as crackpots.

Too much is being taught without enough information, and indeed the wrong information. So where do you start to teach such a big subject?

As with all of the subjects in this book, I can only touch on it lightly, but I hope I will be able to give you a reasonable understanding and lay to rest a few myths and misconceptions. I suppose that before I try to explain what karmic experience is, I need to tell you what it isn't.

I have read many books on the subject, and one in particular stands out in my memory, because I found it hard to swallow. In the book the writer said that if a person became the victim of murder in one life, they would have to meet up with the murderer in a new life. Only this time the murderer would have to become the victim, at the hand of the original victim, in order to understand how it feels to be murdered. This experience would then hopefully teach them not to commit murder again. Of course, this would all be planned out in the spirit world, after life and before the next life on earth. Then came the piece I nearly choked on. With loving spiritual guidance, it would be planned for the victim to take over the role of murderer and then murder the original murderer in the new life. This being a loving act of spiritual kindness, in order that our original murderer might learn a much needed lesson.

Stop right there! I thought. This cannot be right. How can a God of love, who teaches us 'thou shalt not kill', then permit us to kill, in order that someone else can learn a lesson! Didn't the Lord Jesus also say, something like, 'I say *not* an eye for an eye a tooth for a tooth.' Anyway it wasn't very long before I got on the ethereal telephone and asked the Lord to put me right, because I could not accept the theory that this book was trying to sell me. Of course the answer didn't come to me in one quick sentence. Not when an opportunity for me to really learn something was presented. So this information has taken a while to filter through to me over a long period of time. Even now I know what I can tell you is still only a very simplified version. However I can say quite categorically that *no man or woman is ever encouraged to do harm to another, by the spirit world, no matter how much another may need to learn something*.

There is always another and much better way. How can you teach or encourage love if you are hitting someone with a broom handle? By encouraging harm to another, not only are we more likely to instil fear, hatred and resentment, causing more work for the victim, from a need-to-heal point of view, but also the one who did harm, albeit as a means to 'teach and help', will also incur more karmic debt for themselves. They do not become immune even if the intention is to do another a favour, I'm afraid it doesn't work like that. A sin can be washed away, but unless you understand the lesson at heart level, you may very well create similar negative energy again.

As I have said, throughout this book, there is no judgement from God, or anyone in the spirit world. You are not sent back to earth as a punishment and ordered to put right your wrongs, or suffer as a punishment for your crimes. We are compelled to return, by our own thirst for knowledge and quest for enlightenment, and our desire to move on up to the highest levels of consciousness, by giving and receiving love and by being love. Therefore our need to heal and dissolve all negativity is paramount.

It is the negative energy that lives within our energy field that keeps our vibrations on the lower levels of consciousness, and the need to return to earth. By lower levels, I don't mean the dark lower astral planes; I mean the astral planes in general. The astral planes are just one aspect of Heaven. Beyond them is so much more.

You may remember how we talked about like attracting like and how you attract energy to match what exists within your energy field? Well this is very basically what happens. The negative energy within our energy field translates into thoughts and feelings of fear, anger, resentment, distorted beliefs, obsessions. Then we attract situations, opportunities, lessons and people into our lives that correspond to the energy that resonates within our energy field. Because many of our negative attitudes are buried deep within our subconscious we often do not recognise a lesson when it arrives. Instead we react at the seemingly unjust event that is happening in our lives with corresponding negative reaction: with fear, anger, pride, prejudice and resentment a natural reaction. Eventually things calm down and we try to forget about it, but in fact we add more of the same negative energy to the similar energy already within our energy field, making the once small patch of negative energy, even bigger. As this energy becomes bigger, we attract bigger corresponding energy. In other words, when things calm down, and we get on with our life – if we don't drop the event, let go, allow healing and forgiveness, it just gets shelved within our subconscious, until another opportunity presents itself, and we face the same or similar circumstances again, usually more amplified this time. Then our conditioned response rears its head again in reaction to the trigger that activates it.

In time if healing and learning do not take place, our energy may attract more violent conditions to us, or may even manifest itself as a disease within the physical body, or for that matter even our mental body. It is not always important for us to meet people whom we have met in a past life, in order to confront and learn from these lessons, as when the conditions are right, the energy within us reactivates and we attract people and situations toward us who are carrying similar energy within them. At least, where our issue is concerned, in many other ways, we may not have very much in common. Because of this, these people may be likened to ships passing in the night, or a brief encounter.

Mirrors

Whether you are aware of it or not, people are like mirrors, reflecting back to us aspects of *ourselves* all of the time. For instance, you meet someone at a party, and remark to a friend, 'Who does he think he is, he's so self-opinionated.' Of course you may be right, perhaps he is self-opinionated. But if you have the courage to confront yourself, would you not be able to find times, perhaps many times, when you yourself have been very self-opinionated? When we dislike something about someone, it is often a reflection of something we don't admire about ourselves. But it takes a very honest and courageous person to admit that. The good thing about admitting something to yourself is that you don't have to tell anyone else. You can set about changing without anyone else being aware.

Karmic Relationships

Kismet, fate and destiny, we have all heard of one or more of these expressions. When we think of relationships, we tend to think of romantic star-crossed lovers and marriages made in Heaven. Of course marriages are made in Heaven, but these are not always the ideal happily-ever-after type. Granted lots are, but many are not, but that doesn't mean a difficult marriage is a mistake. Indeed, not just the conventional type of marriage is made in Heaven. Choosing to be part of a family is a marriage. Meeting a business partner is a marriage. Your best friend, a teacher and pupil, nurse and patient. All examples of a marriage or a better word may be a contract, an agreement to come together, to work together toward a common goal. We may have unfinished business to work out together, left over from a past life. Or perhaps we have never come together on earth before, but we can both teach and learn from each other. In a way, we are all teachers to each other. We all have something to give and something to gain from all of our associations. But it is our most intimate relationships that offer us the chance to learn our most important lessons. By intimate, I mean those that have the most lasting impact. They are not always the longest associations. After all, you may have a very intense but brief encounter with someone, who perhaps dies early, or goes to live abroad. Your lesson may be to learn to let go, gracefully and with acceptance, honouring the other person rather than resenting them for spoiling your happiness by not staying with you. Power struggles between couples are very common, and there are many, many different issues to be worked out between them. The best way for these to take place are within a relationship of relative permanence, such as a marriage or a long term business partnership, where over the years a great deal of karmic ground can be covered, as transiting conditions offer new and varied opportunities to work things out.

If a couple are fighting like cat and dog on a regular basis, but despite all the odds, stay together to fight another day, you can be sure that their marriage has been 'made in Heaven'. It may not seem likely, but this couple has probably been together many times before. Not necessarily in a marriage situation, but as the negative energy builds up between them, the issues to be worked out between them also build up, until a permanent relationship, such as a marriage, may become the best opportunity to try and work things out for them, so that they may have enough contact. Of course the intention is not to let them bash the living daylights out of each other. A higher plan is worked out very carefully in advance, with spiritual guidance trying to keep us on the higher path. However, free will and the ever-growing negative energies between the couple, means that when they co-create the reality that they live together from moment to moment, via their attitudes, beliefs and feelings, they trigger their conditioned responses. All of the transiting conditions and opportunities offer positive outcomes. A chance for growth, learning, understanding and togetherness. A bonding in love, not acrimony; although it may not seem like it at the time. When we allow our negativity to overwhelm us, we become chained. This chain compels us to return to the karmic wheel, rather than coming together by choice and a bond of love. Instead we are compelled by need, with no choice.

From where we are standing it looks as if our couple never really stood a chance, and yet a lot of careful preparation and pre-life education will have been undergone and much advice and help given. We would not have entered something we could not cope with. Our earth life up to the point of our meeting with our significant partner would have been full of opportunities to learn smaller lessons along the way in preparation for this bigger event. Intuition and conscience are gifts that we all have. We know right from wrong. We feel awful inside if we have a row with a partner. We don't like the atmosphere, so now we have a choice where we can do something positive about it, or we can do something negative. Will we plot revenge, while we seethe with anger, or will we apologise from the heart and try to work things out? When you try open-heartedly, and not with a self-righteous, moralistic attitude, your partner will pick up the vibes and respond accordingly. Quite often it's not just a need to work things out between you. It could be a need to have the courage to confront your faults. Perhaps your partner will point out your faults. But rather than accepting that they could be speaking the truth to you, you strike out with anger and blame, when your partner was only being a mirror for you. When we reach a level of love and respect for our partner, and also for ourselves, faults and all, we will create a new energy within our energy field that says, I love you, I love myself, I'm ready to work on my faults, if you will help me. Your partner picks up the new energy and starts to respond in a new and more loving way.

Of course, there will be hiccups along the way. You will not change all of the negative energy overnight, but your new found determination and enthusiasm for the new lighter love energy will see you through as it starts to get bigger and brighter within you both. As you change, so too does your partner. The best thing is that you are now together by choice and love, not by a compelling need. Or perhaps you choose to part, but you part with honour, respect and love, not because you are exhausted and sick of the sight of each other.

Painful experience, as hard as it may seem, is always our choice, at least subconsciously. Our choice is often masked by things such as fear, pride, prejudice self-righteous superiority. Learning through joy and happiness is always there for the taking, but first we have to be prepared to look at ourselves in a truthful and honest light. To do this we may have to look back at ourselves, our childhood, perhaps even beyond that to a past life experience, whether it be our own or one that parallels our present circumstances. Help on the other side is always available to us; we have only to ask, with a sincere heart. When we ask in this way, we move on to a higher level of consciousness, albeit only temporarily, but it is usually enough to put us in touch with the truth, our higher path and a clearer way forward.

Not all karmic relationships are of a negative kind; indeed many will be a contract of support, help and teamwork.

That Job Had My Name On It!

★

'How did the interview go?'
'Fine, I just knew I'd get the job! It had my name on it.'

Sometimes you just know when you are going to get a particular job, because everything feels right. From a spiritual point of view a job does have your name on it. Certain jobs have

99

been planned for us, because they offer the best opportunities for our spiritual growth. Whether your job is a lifetime vocation or just a stopgap job to tide you over until something better comes along, no opportunity to teach or learn something is ever passed up. A temporary job may be able to prepare you, in some way, for a more important job that you will have in the future. Or perhaps it may give you the opportunity to meet someone who will either play a significant part in your life, or perhaps act as a catalyst between you and something of greater significance to you in the future. Maybe your job will become the stage set for you to work through some unfinished business with someone. Once the work is completed the energy around you changes, and your time within that job comes to an end, unless someone else walks in that you need to meet!

A vocational job may lead you to a life of service where you can learn many lessons, such as compassion, understanding of human nature, learning to honour the many differences that we have, and yet recognising that we are deep down all the same. Perhaps you will be led to give something to the world, or your community, which will bring about many beneficial changes for all concerned. Whilst getting on with your job, you may be unaware of whom you are inspiring. Maybe someone behaves in a jealous way toward you, because you are successful and they want what you have. They want to be like you. Their lesson may be to follow your example, rather than resenting you. There are far too many examples for me to give to you, but if you open your heart and look deeply enough you can usually find the spiritual reasons for why you are in any given situation at any given time. This applies to us from all aspects of life, not just the jobs we find ourselves in. Before we move on, I'd like to share a true story with you from my own experience.

Samantha

I am changing the name of our heroine in this story, to protect her identity. Years ago I worked for a large firm. My job was in printing and copying, a bit monotonous and very repetitive. The company was a large one, with many out stations. One day, I was told that I was being loaned out for a week to one of the out stations. I welcomed the change of scenery and some new faces to get to know. One of those faces was to be Samantha's.

It wasn't long after I arrived that my new colleagues took great delight in telling me all about Samantha.

'Wait till you see her.'

"'It' don't you mean?' called out one of the others.

In actual fact, the man who drove me to work each day had also told me about Samantha, and so it was no surprise to me when my colleagues announced that Samantha was a transexual.

Although I think they were hoping for some kind of shock horror response from me, I just said, 'I know, I've already been told,' and I left it like that. Now don't get me wrong, I got on very well with my new colleagues, in fact one was a boss of mine. In this firm you had many bosses. Another was to become my supervisor, whom I got on very well with. However it wasn't long before the next customer I had to serve was Samantha. Nothing was said, but I guessed that this was Samantha. We chatted politely for a while whilst I did the copying work she requested.

In the background, my colleagues could hardly contain themselves as they held back their titters of laughter. After Samantha left, they burst into an explosion of laughter.

'What's funny, did I miss something?' I asked.

'That was 'it', that was Samantha you were serving.'

I'm not exactly sure of what I said next, but it was something along the lines of, 'I'm well aware of who I was serving, it was obvious.' (Samantha was very big built, not blessed with too many feminine characteristics, like some transexuals).

Then I let rip as they started laughing again.

'You should all be ashamed of yourselves. Samantha is a human being, just like every other customer that comes in here, she deserves to be treated with respect, her sexual inclinations are not anything to do with us. We are here to serve all of our customers, not to treat one with ridicule.'

I must have had a face like thunder. My colleagues appeared frozen in time, their jaws almost on the floor. The silence was so intense, you could feel it.

I went back to my copying machine. As I got on with my work, I was shaking. Crumbs! I had just shouted at the boss! I wondered if I was in deep trouble. I could very easily have been, but I needn't have worried. Very quickly everything returned to normal; nobody said a word to me about the incident. However I gained a great deal of respect. I believe that this incident was the real purpose behind my being loaned out for a week. After all I was called in because they were 'short-staffed' but in fact they were better staffed than my own office. This different job, for just one week, was an opportunity for us all to learn a few spiritual lessons.

I have given several example scenarios to try and help you see how and why we may be keeping ourselves locked within the negative karmic experience. I am very aware at how simple these scenarios may appear, compared to real life experience, which is often more complex. I hope, however, you realise how vast a subject this is to cover, with as many possible scenarios for us to work through, as there are stars throughout our vast universe. But if it only gets you thinking, there is no reason why you can't expand on these ideas yourself.

Prejudice

Supposing you were born into a family where your father was very colour-prejudiced and your mother didn't appear to have an opinion either way, because she was, perhaps, afraid to oppose her husband's view. Remember you chose this family to be born into, because they reflected your own deep-seated prejudice. A past life experience may have been as an eighteenth century slave trader, or perhaps you were a white servant among a household of predominantly black slaves. The past scenario is not important. What is important is that, somehow, you have developed a deep prejudice within you.

Whilst, in your present incarnation, you are subjected to your Dad's comments and attitudes on a regular basis because, like attracts like, you are automatically affected by them, whereas another member of the family may not be (they may have other reasons for being in this family). In this way your past prejudice is reinforced, slowly reawakened and ready to be reactivated at the right time. This is a kind of reminder of what you have come to deal with and heal. You are only affected by the things that you have chosen to deal with in this life; by conditions that you have prearranged such as your birth place and transiting conditions that are planned to the last second. If we had to deal with everything all at once, we'd blow a fuse, so we focus on a few things only in each life.

So now you go to school. A nice small community school that mum and dad approve of. Everything is ticking along nicely when, out of the blue, your family has to move to a different area, which means a different school. In your class are three people from different ethnic backgrounds. They have a different colour skin to you. This is a great environment to work in because you have to go to school. You have to mix with all of your classmates, but you feel odd, strange. All of your prejudice starts to surface. Essentially you are a nice, polite sort of person, so why do you feel this way – uncomfortable, superior, resentful? In front of these three classmates, you try to keep your thoughts and feelings to yourself, but to your best friend, you start making comments to sound him out. But he doesn't support your feelings; neither does he make a big issue out of your comments. Class resumes. The situation is defused for now, but later in the playground, the issue resurfaces, and you start making fun, start rude jokes, trying to encourage your friends. Then one day your best friend has a go at you.

'What's your problem? I think he's a great guy, stop picking on him, you've been making his life a misery lately.'

You skulk away feeling sorry for yourself. What have you done wrong? You were only teasing; can't he take a joke? You are really upset that your best mate isn't speaking to you. Now you feel lonely, isolated, rejected, and unpopular. Before he came along everything was fine. He's twisted you best mate's mind, turned him against you, or so you think. Your prejudice has become stronger, more personal now. It needn't have become such. You could have got to know the lad, made friends, started the healing process in an easy way, without even noticing. Instead you've chosen the hard way, the painful way.

Anyhow, things calm down and eventually you leave school and get a good job. From time to time the issue raises its ugly head, but you're in control, you've got a lid on it! These days you only feel a bit uncomfortable from time to time. You haven't got a problem anyway; they have!

Time goes by, you meet a nice girl and get married. Your best man is your best mate from school days. Your friendship has survived. Nothing can break you. You've always done everything together.

Then one day your friend announces, 'I'm getting married. I want you to be my best man.'

This is news to you.

'You sly old thing you, I didn't know you were even seeing anyone.'

Your friend has been putting off telling you. He still remembers your attitudes, from school days, and since then too. You agree to be best man.

'It will be an honour, congratulations, when do I get to meet the lucky lady?'

'I'll introduce you to her on Saturday, down the pub,' your best friend replies.

When Saturday comes it's shock time. Your best mate is standing with – well 'she's black'.

There must be a mistake. Uncomfortable feelings and confusion start up in you again. You feel numb. You ask yourself why that's a problem, but there isn't time. You are polite but distant. Your mate asks for your opinion and proudly points out how attractive she is. You mumble some trite response.

The next day after you have recovered, and have time to think, you feel it is your duty to point out to your best friend a few things. You wouldn't want him to make a big mistake. After all mixed marriages; they don't really work, do they? So off you go to give your best friend your well-meaning and sincere advice. At first your mate listens kindly and tries to reassure you, but soon your prejudice starts to show. You upset your best friend, who can't see the problem. After all it's his life, and he loves her. But still you go on, until your friend gets really upset. You have a row, and storm out on your best friend, and your long-term friendship is now very fragile to say the least. But, it can be repaired you could say you're sorry, explain your feelings. Perhaps ask your friend to help you or seek some professional help, because you have realised that you have an irrational problem. Or you can carry right on going in the opposite direction. Never to see your friend again, blame him, and his stupid girlfriend.

As you were muttering and moaning to yourself did you feel that sense of déjà vu? Did you recognise that you have been here before? So what is it to be? Correct your prejudice problem by getting to know your best mate's beautiful girlfriend, and, let's face it, she is beautiful, when you take the trouble to get to really know her. You can keep your long-term friendship with your best mate, gain a new friend, and heal a prejudice problem into the bargain! Or you can opt for the miserable painful way again. Lose a best friend; miss out on the opportunity of a new friendship. Things will calm down. You will soon feel better, and you can forget the whole silly incident. That is until you walk into the office of your new highly paid enviable job!

This of course is only an imaginary scenario; whatever specific challenge will confront our bigot is immaterial. The key issue is that there will be continuous opportunities for him to review his actions and learn his spiritual lesson. Only he can decide whether to take advantage of them.

Retribution

I was watching one of those debate-type chat shows on television. It was entitled 'I can't get over being mugged'.

In the audience, of course, were many angry and bitter people, who had suffered at the hands of a mugger, or had a loved one who had been. In the audience also was a young man who had been a mugger. He had committed the crime with the help of a friend on two occasions. It was obvious to me that this young man really regretted doing what he had done and had come onto the show, (a very brave act on his part) to try to do something toward making amends, by discouraging others from doing the same as he had.

I say that he was brave, because all of the people, who had been victim to a mugging, targeted all of their anger and bitterness at this young man. He didn't try to defend himself, but kept saying that he was sorry and that he had learned his lesson. All of his body language was that of a contrite man, but the victims of muggings (not at the hands of this young man) were too angry and bitter to believe he meant it. Of course what he did, and many others just like him, is wrong. These people do need to be taught a lesson. But if we are the victims of their crime, we are not the appropriate people to judge the nature of the punishment and lesson required. I understand that the victims of crime feel much pain, anguish, fear and a desire for justice. That is only normal. It goes with the experience. But when justice becomes a desire for retribution, something different is happening. When fear and anger are held on to for years, when they dominate your life, distortion and corrosion will set in. We will never forget the painful and terrifying experiences that happen in our life, but we shouldn't allow them to cripple us. During the television show, many people said that not only could they not forget their experience, but also then they went on to say that, they could never live a normal life again. They would live with their fear for the rest of their lives, and other similar statements.

But why? Why be a victim all of your life? Why let one bad experience control and manipulate you and spoil the rest of your life? Why set yourself up to attract more of the same, or similar in the future? (Several people commented that they had been a victim of mugging on more than one occasion).

Do you have to wear a label marked *victim* for the rest of your life? Of course not, you can take it off, if you want to. The choice is yours, and you have free will. Of course it will take courage. It may not be easy; perhaps you will need some kind of therapy to help you achieve freedom, but what a triumph. Just think of what you can gain!

Perhaps you hope the mugger will suffer, if they know that you are suffering and that your life is ruined? Where is the mugger now? Long gone. They may not see you again. If they learn from their mistakes, it will probably be from their consciences preying on their minds, not by your continued self-punishment of fear and dread that they will be unlikely to see.

Many people do not realise that to hold on to fear, anger and resentment is to make yourself a victim. What you give out, you get back eventually, because as I have said many times, like attracts like. If you light a fire, it burns. When you add more fuel to it, it continues to burn. When you stop feeding the fire it will eventually go out. It's the same with our thoughts. The more you entertain fear, the greater your fear becomes, and the bigger your fear gets, the more likely you are to attract fearful events into your life, not to mention the misery that your fearful thoughts cause you at the time. When we think negatively we are laying ourselves wide open. By the same token, thoughts of bitterness and anger set you up for corrosion and distortion. Gradually your physical body starts to deteriorate, you become ill with disease. You are sick and tired of the fear and the misery running through your mind. Anger and bitterness destroy the beauty of who and what you are.

When you keep thinking hurtful angry thoughts about the mugger, you keep reliving the experience. Before long you are in a prison of your own making. The more thoughts you give out, the more negative energy you attract back. Everything is amplifying. You are constantly miserable. You feel crippled and broken.

You tell people, 'The mugger did this to me.'

Compassionately, I would say that I'm afraid you are wrong. Whilst the mugger gave you the initial experience, you are the one who continues the humiliation. In all experience is the opportunity to grow and learn spiritually, whether it was an experience we needed to have, or not, (we put ourselves through much unnecessary torment). But how you react to the experience after the event is entirely up to you. Of course, given similar circumstances, we would all be shaken up, frightened, confused and angry. That is only natural. But how long will we choose to allow ourselves to be dominated by fear, anger, bitterness and resentment? How long will we choose to corrode our minds, and bodies? Constant anguish can lower our immune systems and lay us open to illness, be it colds or cancer. When will we allow ourselves to be more positive and loving towards ourselves? Not all illness is attributed to negative emotions, but much of it is. Don't you owe it to yourself to love yourself enough, to let go of the past and start living again, and enjoy a quality life, with the freedom to please yourself, free from fear.

Perhaps you think it's easy for me to say these things, but believe me I've had my share of hurt too. Retribution is not the way forward. The 'eye for an eye, a tooth for a tooth' kind of mentality keeps us going round in circles on the karmic wheel. I can highly recommend self-love and forgiveness.

Disabilities

Every Wednesday I like to go swimming with a friend. On this particular day we were running late. We were keen to hurry up and change, so that we could have a good swim before the session ended. We were busy shovelling our clothes into the tiny lockers, when we heard someone sobbing. My friend went to investigate and we found a young woman standing helplessly looking on at her friend, who was sitting in the cubicle sobbing. Not wishing to interfere, we tentatively asked if the girl needed any help. The young woman hastily explained what had just happened. Her friend Janet (name changed) had been swimming, the front crawl, and was told off and called a big fat blubbering whale who had no business being in the water, splashing and making such a mess. Janet had a disabled hip, and the front crawl was the only way she could swim. I went to sit with Janet and quietly talked to her, explaining that she had as much right to be in the water as anyone else, that it was a freestyle part of the pool, so she could do the front crawl if she wanted, but most of all she shouldn't allow others to victimise her. I suspected that Janet had been a victim of similar abuse before and told her so. She replied that she had, and because of this she had stopped going to other social gatherings, or sports activities, because she felt hounded. I suggested to Janet that it was time for things to change, that she should take the plunge, and get back into the water today. I invited her to come into the water with my friend and myself, which I am glad to say she did and she still swims fairly regularly now.

On this day the story had a happy ending for Janet, but it could have been the same as other times, miserable and painful. This time, however, Janet acted boldly. She overcame the disability in her mind. You see, although Janet had been born with defective hips, and had undergone many operations as a child, this was not the real disability. Janet is married, has children, and lives a very normal life, doing lots of things other mums do with their children. Janet's physical disability was a catalyst, to help her to wake up to a spiritual truth, perhaps to reach a new understanding. I say, perhaps, because I do not know Janet that well, nor can I know her spiritual path, but perhaps Janet is trying to learn self worth. To be more assertive (not aggressive). To learn to stick up for herself and say, 'I have as much right as the next person. I am worthy, I have beauty in my own right.'

So why would Janet's lesson be so drastic as to need a physical defect? Well, in the first place, she would not have needed such drastic measures, but remember how like attracts like, and how we draw energy to us, to match what already exists within us. Well, this is what happens when we don't learn something and the healing process is prevented. We keep attracting more dark negative energy, creating a bigger patch of dark energy within our energy field. If you could see the energy field it is like a multi-coloured egg surrounding us, changing with our moods and spiritual evolution. Dark negative energy sits in the energy field like a dark, dirty stain, or a black blob. When this energy is added to, it grows bigger. What started out as negative energy, in just the mental body, has progressed to the emotional body and from there it will spread into the etheric energy body, which is the exact replica of the physical body. This may take several lifetimes to develop. Once energy has reached this level, it is only a matter of time before it will manifest itself in the physical, and that means it could translate into a disease, or a physical defect.

Therefore we attract corresponding conditions in the physical world. When a person is born with a defect, they have attracted those conditions to themselves. It isn't a punishment for 'past sins', as has been suggested by many who teach about reincarnation. It's just that, as negative energy grows bigger within us, we are compelled always to attract similar energy, like magnets. It is only when we transmute the negative energy within us, by overcoming problems, and start healing, that we stop attracting such negative energy which in its turn translates into negative conditions on earth.

We are aware, before we come to earth, that we have negative energy within our energy field that needs changing. We are well aware of the conditions that we will inevitably attract when we choose to deal with an old hurt or problem. Of course we do not deal with all of our problems and hang-ups in one life, because it would be too distracting. Therefore only energy that corresponds to our chosen transiting conditions will be reactivated, in other words via our pre-planned life plan.

Collective Karma

Isn't it funny how you can show your son or daughter your wedding photos one day and they make comments such as, 'Dad looks ridiculous in that suit, those flared trousers and long hair. How could you wear that suit – and on you're wedding day too!'

A couple of years later flares are back in fashion. 'I thought you said flares looked stupid, a couple of years ago,' you may comment.

'No I didn't; besides they're in now, it's what everybody is wearing now – at least anyone who isn't over the hill, like you.'

They mean anyone who has had the misfortune to have turned twenty-five! And even though you and your generation declared flares out of fashion in 1980 and wouldn't be seen dead in a pair now, according to your teenage offspring, they are 'cool', the must-have item, along with 1970s music, glossy lipstick and soppy blouses with big-tie bows. And how could I forget the all-essential platform shoes?

So why does this sort of thing happen? Suddenly shops the world over are flooded with 1970s clothing and music, almost identical to the stuff we gave away to charity shops years ago. A designer presents his or her idea to the influential fashion promoters and, before you know it, the shops are flooded. But why do all of the teenagers want the look suddenly? Why don't some choose to be more individual, or choose a different style, say 1940s or 1920s? Why do they all wear the same things? Granted, fashion dictatorship and the media have a lot to do with it. But just because something is in fashion doesn't mean that we all have to like it. So what is happening? There is a collective consciousness at work here amongst teenagers. Once the first idea has broken through the first barrier, it isn't long before it filters through and spreads like an epidemic.

The way we think and feel as a society helps to shape the

world we live in. Just as you create your individual world with your thoughts, feelings and attitudes, albeit consciously or unconsciously, we also create the wider world, by the way we all think as a collective.

One day two Jehovah Witnesses visited me and asked if there was anything missing from my life.

'If you mean God, no he isn't missing from my life,' I replied.

Naturally this led to a long conversation. One of the ladies then asked me, how I felt about the terrible world we live in and the dreadful things that were happening all around us. I then told her that half of the trouble and the reason for the so-called dreadful world we live in, is that as a collective, we thought too much in terms of the negative, instead of the positive, that we should be focusing on the way we would like our world to be and, in our own small way, make our personal contribution toward that effort. I then went on to explain a little about cause and effect, and how your thoughts were energy that stayed in the ether and grew if similar thoughts were added on a regular basis. How, eventually, our thoughts would manifest themselves in the physical world, in other words, they become the world we live in. The lady asked me if I thought I was being unrealistic. I said, 'No, because the reality of our tomorrow starts with our thoughts today. I realise that today I maybe thinking alone, but you are welcome to join me with your own positive thoughts. The responsibilities lie with all of us.'

I'd like to share an example. Every year we honour the dead, who died for us in the two World Wars, and subsequent wars, with poppies. Poppies have come to symbolise the many sacrifices that were made and gave those who had lost friends and family the opportunity to honour their memory. It is only right that such noble acts should be recognised. Yet in effect the poppy and Remembrance Day initially bring to mind death, loss, anguish, war, cruelty and dominance. By repeatedly focusing on these issues, negative emotions come to the fore. On a mass level this creates a pool of negative energy, which allows similar events to recur in the future. There has to come a time when these events are put behind us and the focus is placed on a peaceful future and how it can be achieved. Many died for the sake of a just peace. Can we really say that we are working toward this? There is no disrespect to the many who died, in that people will still have their individual memories, regardless.

Perhaps we could find a new way to honour those who made their sacrifices for us, with events that bring us closer together and encourage us to unite in thoughts of peace, love and tolerance.

Throughout this book I have tried to get across to you the power of your thoughts, feelings, attitudes, and beliefs, and how these things are the energy that attracts like energy toward you. In this way we are constantly creating the world that we live in. We have an enormous amount of power at our fingertips, if we would but realise it. If you don't like the world you are living in, you, and you alone, have the power to change your world for a better one. Our bigger world, however, is up to us all.

It may not change as fast as it will in the spirit world, but it will change, if you put *your mind to it*. You are not a victim of circumstances. God is not punishing you. It may be fairer to say that we are all victims of ourselves, we are all harming ourselves in one way or another. We are responsible for ourselves, the world we choose to experience, as well as that which we contribute to the lives of all those that we come into contact with.

As our souls gain experience, our consciousness expands, all of our experiences are stored within our ever-expanding consciousness and we are constantly refining and improving ourselves. Our personalities are a mixture of strengths and weaknesses. It is our job to turn weaknesses into strengths, not to bury them or despise them, but work with them, transmute them from negative to positive energy. I once saw a great title for a book, called, 'It is not my fault I'm a Gemini'.

There are no excuses. Leopards can change their spots, if they want to. It is no good saying I can't help myself, it's part of my nature, it's the way I was brought up, or I'm no worse than anyone else. These and other excuses we come up with are just masks to hide behind. After all, it's easier to hide behind a bush than to have the courage to come out and face up to one's responsibilities, and oneself. It won't be an easy ride to begin with, but it will get better as you go along. So do yourself a favour; start taking responsibility for yourself and your world. Give yourself the gift of freedom, from the ever-turning wheel of negative karmic experience and start experiencing the wonder of life!

Chapter Ten
DISEASE

ONE OF THE QUESTIONS THAT I AM ASKED A LOT IS, 'IF GOD is such a loving God, why does he allow us to become ill?' As you might expect, the answer isn't a simple one, at least not in one sentence. But, before we launch forth into the deeper understanding of the answer, the simple answer is, yes you've guessed it, God doesn't interfere with our free will, and *we* allow *ourselves* to get sick. Then, the next question is why on earth would we want to do that? Of course it does seem rather crazy, but, by now, you should be getting the hang of things and perhaps you can more or less work out the answer for yourself.

As we explore a deeper understanding, it should be remembered that everybody is a unique individual and, therefore, there is no one reason for sickness. No two people will experience disease and sickness in the same way, even if they have the same illness and the same symptoms. In other words every illness is as unique as the individual. Therefore you cannot justifiably say all people who get cancer, get it because of A, or all people who get arthritis get it because of B, because it doesn't work like that, at least not from a spiritual point of view.

Of course all diseases are subject to the law of cause and effect, but some things appear to be obvious, whilst others seem not to have any rhyme or reason, and you are left wondering, why have you been dealt such a cruel fate? Why me? Why this? What have I done to deserve this? When we say things like that we are generally feeling understandably very sorry for ourselves, frightened probably, and if the truth were known, we are looking for someone to blame. Quite often it is God. If God is so wonderful and he loves me like they say he does, why does he let me get sick? If he cares why doesn't he make me better? Never once do we think that perhaps in some way, we might be to

113

blame. Maybe we should consider that. When we understand the deeper meaning of disease, we start to realise that we are responsible, not only for our lives, but also for our own diseases.

Now I know not every case can be put under the same roof so to speak, nor shall I attempt to do that. It is not my task to judge, but hopefully to bring insight, or at least a little more insight!

Over the aeons of time, man has weakened the physical DNA structure through personal and collective karma. Disease will be with us until the balance is restored. A physical manifestation, such as a disease, is the outward expression of karmic imbalance. Just as our body can produce illness in response to disharmony, it can also produce a state of complete healing and recovery. Complete, if you can believe enough and allow a state of harmony and rebalance. For most people this is still a difficult concept to understand, especially during a time of threat. This has largely happened because of the state of the collective consciousness. However, gradually a new level of consciousness will emerge, as new understanding starts to get a grip.

When a soul descends to earth, it agrees to a whole package, so to speak. When we choose our parents, we also accept the ancestral genetic makeup, and the predisposition to the diseases inherent within the ancestral line. However, because like attracts like, we may only be affected by a disease if we have unhealed issues that correspond to the energy inherent within the weakness of the DNA structure, whilst another member of our family, who perhaps does not share all of the same issues as us, will not be affected.

Having said this, it is never a foregone conclusion that we will contract a disease that has been handed down through the generations if we do the work that we came here to do successfully. That is to say, if we deal with our issues, finish unfinished business, forgive, apologise, heal, create harmony, then we need not contract a disease. But we should not forget collective karma. We may have dealt with our personal issues successfully, but what if we are gripped with fear or by a collective belief? For example: 'If your family has an inherited disease, then the odds are that you are bound to get it as well eventually, because a lot of the women in your family have already succumbed to that fate.'

Or, 'It seems to affect every other generation, and now it's your generation. That means the finger is pointing at you.'

'Well isn't it?' That kind of fear is so destructive. In this way people suffer disease needlessly.

It is not possible to explain all that there is to know about disease. But, broadly speaking, disease is either personal or collective in its action. Being born with a diseased body does not mean that the person must have been really wicked in a past life. Before stones are cast, let us remember that we are *all* working out karmic imbalance in our lives, in some way or another, and we are dealing with as much as we can cope with at this time. I cannot give you a reason why one person experiences horrendous disease, pain and suffering, as each soul's experience is unique to them.

As with the last chapter, this is difficult to explain in full because, karmic experience is as vast as the universe. However I will present several scenarios to give a better idea of how disease maybe awakened within us, or be attracted to us.

A Love Story

Our story begins, for Marjorie and Ken, back in the fifties, when Elvis was top of the charts – 'Sorry! I mean top of the hit parade!' DAs were all the rage; CDs were not even a twinkling of an eye. Frothy coffee and Danset record players ruled the waves. 'The good old days', when men were men, and women stayed home, doing housework, and had babies! This is when Marjorie and Ken fell in love and became an item – 'Oh sorry! I mean, they started courting.' Then came marriage and babies, two actually, a boy and a girl, a happy marriage, well… it was wonderful in the early days, until Ken got his first promotion. To be fair Ken did very well. One promotion led to another and he provided a good home for Marjorie and the kids. She didn't have to go to work; she had everything that she needed. The trouble was that wasn't how Marjorie saw things. Marjorie cooked and cleaned and Ken was at work. He was always at work. They never did anything together anymore.

In fact, she hardly saw Ken these days. It's not that Ken was a bad man. Marjorie still loved him. It was just, well, he never noticed her anymore. However he soon noticed if dinner wasn't on the table on time. If only he had phoned! After all how was she to know that he was coming home early? In fact Ken took his wife very much for granted. The crisp white shirts neatly packed for yet another business trip abroad. Dinner for six business colleagues at the drop of a hat.

'I know it's short notice,' he would say, 'but you're a wonder in the kitchen Marge, you'll manage somehow. I've got to go now, Mr Stephens has arrived.' And somehow Marjorie did always manage. But she resented it, the assumption and everything. At least she always got flowers on her birthday, and yet, somehow, it wasn't the same, getting a general mixed bouquet that his secretary had organised for her each year. Did he still love her? In the old days he'd send her red roses, or orchids, even though he could ill-afford it. Was there someone else? She dismissed that idea; he was too busy.

If Marjorie broached the subject, Ken would naturally become defensive.

'I've been very busy – you know how it is – you've got a lovely home, haven't you? I pay all the bills. You don't have to work, and I'm a good provider aren't I?'

Marjorie always had to agree. She couldn't fault him there. It was just the way he never noticed her, took her for granted and expected her to drop everything at a moment's notice and let her down time after time after time. She had no life of her own; she felt neglected and unappreciated, unloved. The bloom had gone from her face.

Perhaps if I lost a little weight, she thought. So she did. She smartened herself up, took up art classes. Ken didn't notice her weight loss, but Mike, his colleague from work did, but Marjorie wasn't interested in having an affair. She still loved Ken, but heaven only knew why. The art classes didn't please Ken either. Where was Marjorie when he needed her? It was too inconvenient. Why did she want to paint at her age?

Marjorie thought she would try pointing out her weight loss to Ken. He'd be proud of her when he realised. They would go out to dinner, a nice quiet little restaurant. She would wear that blue dress he liked so much, now she could get back in to it once more. Marjorie's heart skipped a beat and she started to sing as she swanned around the room like a lovesick schoolgirl. But Ken's response was like a slap round the face with a wet rag!

'Oh yes dear, very nice dear, well done, well done indeed,' he absentmindedly muttered, as he looked for his glasses.

Marjorie wouldn't have minded, but he didn't even look at her.

'And Saturday?' she called out, hopefully.

'Sorry, Marge, no can do, president of the company is coming.' His voice trailed off into the distance as he strode off toward the potting shed.

Not for the first time Marjorie felt dismissed like an office junior. Perhaps some sexy underwear – yes! No, she'd tried that before.

She had even tried leaving Ken once. He'd begged her to come back. She did and within a week everything was back to normal, that is to say, Ken's promise, to try harder, had been filed away in some ethereal filing cabinet. Over the years Marjorie had tried many things, from gentle hints, to frank chats at the kitchen table. A bouquet of flowers would turn up, no doubt arranged by the secretary.

Then one day Marjorie wasn't at home when Ken came home unexpectedly. He was in a hurry. Where was the infernal woman? He couldn't be late for the meeting. He had to catch the plane on time. He'd left a message on the answer machine, warning her that he needed a suitcase packed and he'd be home to collect it, and that was hours ago. She knew it was important, where was she? He'd just have to do it himself. If he forgot something important… Ken muttered on and on to himself. Blast the woman! His shirts weren't ironed. What was she playing at?

Just as Ken was whipping himself up into a frenzy, Marjorie walked in through the door; her tear-stained face pale and ashen. In a daze, she walked toward Ken.

'Where have you been, I've only got an hour,' he started. 'I'm in a hurry. Did you get my suit from the cleaners, the black one?'

'No Ken,' Marjorie began, in a voice barely audible. 'I've been to the doctors. I have cancer. The doctor thinks it is too advanced for surgery. He thinks I've only got about six months left.' She couldn't bring herself to say, 'to live'. In the deathly silence that followed, Ken dropped his socks to the floor. The colour now drained from his face, as he stared at his wife and tried to comprehend what she has just told him.

'What did you just say?' For the first time in years Marjorie had finally got Ken's full attention, only now she could hardly speak, her lip trembled, and years of pent up emotion, as well as shock from the news, came to the surface and she burst into tears, that tumbled down her face. Ken was rooted to the spot. But, somehow, he found the courage to take his wife in his arms and held her trembling body. For what seemed a long time they just held each other. Then tenderly he sat his wife down on the bed.

'I won't go to Brussels. I'll send someone else.'

From now on a great change was going to take place in Ken and Marjorie's life. Ken decided to take care of Marjorie. He'd go to the hospital with her, take care of her at home, take her out when she was well enough. He would go and see his boss, explain the situation, and get all the compassionate leave that he needed. This was now possible, because the personality was in harmony with soul desire, and could easily attract what was needed. So Ken's work was redirected.

For the first time in years, Ken was spending quality time with his wife. They were talking, sharing, caring, giving, receiving. Love was blossoming once more. Ken told Marjorie that he loved her, and Marjorie with tears in her eyes told Ken she had always loved him. These last six months had been the happiest of their lives, save for the sickness, and weakness that Marjorie was experiencing. Ken became more and more devoted. He spent time cooking and cleaning and realised how much his lovely wife did for him. His love and appreciation were growing more and more each day.

The final day came around, far too soon, Marjorie looked tired, pale, her eyes were sunken, and she was very weak. Now the morphine meant that she seemed drugged up to the eyes, and yet, when Ken looked into the eyes of his lovely wife, in those last few minutes, he thought that Marjorie's eyes had never looked so beautiful. He had seen the love of her soul, as her hand went limp, and she quietly slipped away. Ken knew in his heart, as he softly cried at the loss of his wife, that love is the most important and precious thing about life.

Although Marjorie died from her disease, she did not die in vain. Part of her spiritual mission was fulfilled. She helped Ken to learn to appreciate and to love. He realised how important love is, and about the need for balance in our lives. Marjorie's soul took advantage of the disease that was growing in her body, and used it as a tool for learning and teaching. Marjorie's and Ken's love was strengthened considerably, because of the experience that they shared.

However, it could have happened differently. For instance, if Marjorie had examined herself more closely and worked on building self-esteem, her energy would have changed her to a self-confident, self-respecting woman. And Ken's reactions to Marjorie would have changed also. His respect for his wife would have increased. He would have seen her in a different light. Since his reactions were also more positive, Marjorie would continue to strengthen. The interaction between them would have grown more positive. Their time together would have become happier and longer. Marjorie would not have developed the disease, which stemmed from her unhappiness and lack of self-esteem. If Ken and Marjorie had walked this path, all of the spiritual goals that they set out to achieve together could have been accomplished; as not only would Ken have learned about appreciation and love, but also, Marjorie would have learned about self-esteem and self-love. Also it could all have been achieved without pain and suffering.

Marjorie will have another chance to learn about self-esteem in the future, but for now she and Ken can treasure all that they gained together, albeit in a sad and painful way.

A Call to Responsibility

Julie is a pretty woman in her early thirties. She is a successful businesswoman, a journalist. She's reached a senior position, and is doing very well. Her job gives her a great adrenaline rush, the travel, the parties. She has a husband, a little girl of four years old, a nice home and car. Her mother looks after her daughter until her husband gets home. Her mother cooks tea most evenings for her husband and daughter. It's unfortunate, but often little Gemma is asleep in bed when Julie gets home from work. But Julie loves her little daughter. She looks so sweet with her blonde curls falling gently around her face. Julie would like to spend more time with her daughter, but it's her work. She has to work. She wants her daughter to go to the best school next year, and that costs money. Her husband's income isn't that good. In truth her husband's money is very good. Julie needs to make excuses for herself. She likes her job, and, besides, why should she be the little woman at home?

But Julie is getting tired, really tired. At first she puts it down to too many late nights. She's only thirty-something.

'This is ridiculous, at my age,' she said, 'I need to get fit.'

So she joins a gym and adds a fitness regime to her already punishing schedule. She swallows vitamins and orange juice in the mornings, and wine in a smoky wine bar in the evening. Then, one day at a conference, Julie collapses. A colleague helps her to a chair, but Julie is not at all well. An ambulance takes her to the local hospital. Her husband is called. He arrives some three hours later, having driven most of the afternoon, to be with her. Julie has tests and is kept in for observation, she feels better by morning, but the hospital advise her to go to her GP as soon as possible. They will be sending the test results there. Naturally Julie and her husband are concerned. So Julie goes to her doctor. The news is bad. Julie has cancer, and it is fairly well advanced. It is treatable and she has been given a fifty-fifty chance of survival, if she agrees to the treatment. Julie agrees.

Suddenly her mind is flooded with fears and strong emotions. What if she dies? What will happen to Gemma? She may never see her daughter grow up! This idea hits home to Julie with such blunt force, that the tears start to stream down her face. As she sobs to herself on her bed, clutching her knees to her chin, the healing process slowly begins to start, as Julie decides, 'I'm going to live, for my daughter's sake, I'm going to see her grow up.'

With determination in her heart, Julie also decides, she is going to be a proper mother, spend time with her daughter, look after her, as well as herself. That's important too, or how else can she expect to look after Gemma! Julie wants to love her properly. She talks to her husband, and asks him if he would mind if she gave up her job. He tells her, of course not. All he wants is for Julie to be well again so they can be a proper family. So, with his blessing, Julie feels strangely light-hearted, as she picks up the phone and tells her boss that she is handing in her notice.

Despite the chemotherapy, which makes her feel sick and weak, her heart is lighter; she's enjoying her daughter's company, and her loving attention. Her mum still looks after Gemma, when Julie is ill, or at the hospital, only now her mum isn't resentful. She's glad to help, but, naturally, her mum is worried about her own little girl. But she needn't be. Julie is getting better, the chemotherapy seems to be working. In actual fact, the chemotherapy is working because Julie is in harmony with her soul desire. Julie is no longer on a path that will lead to self-destruction. Therefore her energy field is no longer producing the negative energy that will eventually manifest itself as cancer cells in her body. So the chemotherapy can mop up the damage that has already been caused to the physical. Julie is feeling more hopeful. Everyday she feels stronger, she's enjoying her life, and is strangely more peaceful and serene, despite the fact that she has a threatening disease. Gemma is a handful, and Julie still gets very tired, but she's got all the help of a loving family. At last the doctor tells her that her cancer is in remission. She will still need to take drugs and continue to take things easy, one step at a time. As Julie leaves the doctor's surgery, she lifts her head to Heaven and gives a word of thanks to God. She's got her life back and it feels so good.

Nine months ago things looked bleak for Julie. A fifty-fifty chance the doctor had said. She was lucky. Many people don't get so lucky. She could have died, never seen her daughter grow up, never enjoyed such a loving family life, so why did Julie get so lucky? After all, couldn't Julie's death give some special spiritual lesson to her family? Well, yes it could, everyone can gain from all experiences, but Julie's spiritual goal was to learn to take responsibility for her daughter, to teach her, nurture her and to give unselfishly, to put her husband and daughter before herself.

It's not that Julie doesn't deserve happiness for herself; of course she does. But in order to enjoy true happiness, she must first learn to put those that are important to her first, in so doing, her own reward comes to her naturally.

If Julie had not learned her spiritual lesson, she would have surely died and, in the spirit world, she would have realised that she did not learn her lesson. Not only that, but she would have left a daughter without a mother, and a husband and her own mother with the added burden of bringing up her daughter. This then would have become a karmic debt that Julie had incurred. She would have had to try and put things right in the future.

Before we go on, I just want to say that there are many people with children, who get sick, who are determined to beat the illness and to stay because they too want to look after their children, and yet, they still loose the battle. It should not be a forgone conclusion, that death means failure. Please remember that each case is unique, and individual, but also it is important to recognise that being positive and determined to win is not always enough. Being positive includes having the courage to examine ourselves honestly, deeply and at subconscious level, to find the wounds that have injured the soul. To perhaps also be willing to be willing to make some very drastic life changes.

Forgiveness Not Pride

One day, a young woman turned up on my doorstep, in the hope that reflexology would be able to help her. She told me that she was suffering very badly with stress, insomnia, headaches, bowel problems, and various other niggly ailments. On the surface of things reflexology seemed like a very good idea, so I began with reflexology, knowing that the underlying cause of her problems would soon manifest itself as she got to know me and began to talk. Sure enough everything began to tumble out.

This young lady had been living in Australia with her partner and life was very good. They had their own business, and they were doing very nicely, so nicely in fact that the authorities got suspicious.

To cut a long story short, they were not paying taxes. They got into a lot of trouble, and were very lucky not to get a prison sentence.

However they lost everything and were sent back to England, tails between their legs, and were not allowed to return to Australia again. Naturally it isn't unreasonable for anyone to feel sorry for themselves if they found themselves in similar circumstances. Neither is anger, resentment or bitterness an unnatural emotion. The problem starts when you hang on to this kind of energy beyond a reasonable length of time. This young lady was doing just that. The event was over and done with several years ago, but still it was eating at her. Only now, and she couldn't seem to see this very well, something similar was beginning to happen all over again. Her partner had also been angry in the beginning, but had gradually started to let go and get on with building a new life for himself. However our young lady was not letting go. She was very much stuck in the past. She was beginning to lose her partner because they were always arguing about this matter and the strain was beginning to show in their relationship, as well as in her physical body.

I tried to explain very gently that she needed to let go of the past and start again, like her partner. If she did she could start to rebuild a new life. Her relationship would improve. Her health would improve. She could be happy again. I talked at great length; I offered her spiritual healing to help her with the necessary attitude change she would need, but to no avail. This young lady wanted her old life given back to her. She wanted me to pity her and somehow support her crusade. She said that she would have the healing so long as God could help give her life back and fight this injustice on her behalf. I tried to explain, but she couldn't see that not paying taxes is also an injustice to Australia. That she had been treated justly in the circumstances. Now it was time for her to learn and move on. She accused me of being the same as all the rest and I never saw her again. I don't know if she ever learned the much needed lesson. I hope she did, before it was too late. I knew it would be the only way that her world would improve in every aspect, but I suspect she did not; at least not right away. How much further damage she did to her health and relationship is hard to say, but it was obvious that her partner was beginning to move on. His energy had changed; he would feel compelled to move on sooner or later. Would his partner go with him? The choice was in her hands, but without the much-needed change of attitude the painful lesson was beginning all over again. The first time she lost her business. This time she looked set to lose a good relationship and perhaps, her home and health. All that was needed was acceptance and forgiveness, not pride.

Enjoying Bad Health

Some people seem to enjoy bad health. I say enjoy; that isn't really true, but they go on about it so much it seems that way. To be fair their illnesses are a cover up for a much deeper problem. The illness, and the attention it brings, is a form of protection and they subconsciously feel the need for it. What they really need is to address the problem, I'll give two examples.

A man I know has many ailments of various kinds. Every time I see him and ask how he is he tells me in great detail. In the early days of our acquaintance I tried to help him, by offering reflexology, which he came for and enjoyed. However, I got to the real problem and discovered that not only was he a widower and lived alone, his family hardly ever came to see him and they sounded like a very cold callous bunch. In fairness to his family, I had never met them, and have never heard their side of the story. However, this man was a very lonely man, with very few real friends, so consequently had few visitors. One saving grace was his ability to drive. He still drives now, even though he is in his eighties. He has a reasonable pension, so I suggested that he might try going to evening classes, to make new friends. Then came the excuses. I made other suggestions, but to no avail.

'But if you feel that lonely,' I said, 'I know it takes courage to walk into somewhere new for the first time, but you'd feel so much happier with new friends. If you don't like evening classes because of the dark, (a reason he gave me for not going) why not go during the day? There are lots to choose from.'

But he never went. Rather than meet the challenge and doing something about his loneliness, he prefers to stay home attracting illness, in the hope that sympathy will come to him. This only gives temporary relief to him, as it doesn't really address the real issue.

Another example is that of a married woman whose husband is going away on a business trip. She suddenly develops an illness, yet yesterday she was fine. This happens every time he has to go away. He gets impatient. In the early days he was really concerned and phoned his wife regularly to check that she was all right. But, now it's not that he doesn't believe that she was sick this morning; he knows she was, he's sorry for her, but it happens every time he goes away. She's always fine when he comes back and it's getting a bit wearing, because he's made to feel guilty. It's his job for heaven's sake.

Impatiently he says, 'I've got to go, I'll ring you later. If you continue to feel bad, call your sister.'

He hurries away feeling stressed and depressed. He's tried asking her what is wrong. Is something bothering her? Doesn't she trust him? Is that it?

She smiles weakly and says that isn't it. She lowers her eyes as she quietly says, 'Of course I trust you.'

The truth is she doesn't trust him, even though there hasn't been any hint of suspicion, and deep down she knows she should trust him. He's a good man. In actual fact it's her that is the problem. She is jealous, and conjures up all sorts of possible scenarios between her husband and an imaginary woman, which stem from deep feelings of insecurity. This is the real issue that needs addressing. This is what needs healing. By facing up to the fact and seeking help to overcome and heal the problem is the spiritual challenge to be met. Her sickness, each time her husband goes away, is the physical expression to gain attention, so that help and healing can be found; a sort of cry for help, to free her soul from this negative energy, which cripples her with fear.

For this woman, her sickness brings her husband's attention back to her. This then alleviates the fear and insecurity for a while, but when he no longer responds, the need to create more violent illness becomes a real possibility. If real help for the real problem isn't found, then the danger of a major disease is more and more possible. We keep re-enacting the same things in our lives over and over, because we are trying to achieve healing, and true understanding. Our loved ones keep going over the same act with us, in the hope that we eventually get it right. But some times our loved ones need to move on without us, if necessary. If we don't learn the lesson, we may blame our loved one for needing to go on, and see this instead, as someone who doesn't care about us. This then adds more energy to the existing negative energy within us that in this case is reflected by insecurity and feelings of irrational jealousy. Consequently there is a harder lesson to confront in the future.

Hypochondria

Hypochondria is a sickness that causes real sickness, constant worry, fear and negative thinking that eventually creates the very illnesses that have been feared and worried about. Not to mention the lowering of the immune system, which makes you more susceptible to all of the bugs and viruses that are going around. People who suffer with hypochondria have their imaginations running wild. They quite often will keep some kind of medical or herbal reference book to look up symptoms. They always think the worst and their imagination puts them through hell. The physical body is in a constant state of stress, which then encourages a release of excess uric acid that can often result in arthritis. Before we go on, I'm not suggesting all cases of arthritis are caused by hypochondria. Many people with varying degrees of hypochondria can create all sorts of illness. The real issue here is what has caused the hypochondria in the first place.

I see many clients with genuine illness, but I am aware that a lot of people I see have problems that are caused by constant worry, fear and negative thinking, their minds going into overdrive. They are exhausted and tearful. They have so many things wrong with them it's a wonder that they can function at all. Of course I cannot correct irreparable damage. As an aromatherapist and reflexologist, I am happy to say that over the years, I have been able to help many people with many different problems. But when I recognise that a person is the creator of their many problems, with constant worry, fear and negative thinking and talking about their various ongoing illnesses and ailments, I realise that any treatment I can offer will only bring them temporary relief.

So I have started to include a new programme for them. This is a programme of positive thinking, perhaps the writing down of affirmations. Watching funny videos (known to raise the immune system). I ask them to write down the good things in their life, to help them change their focus from worry to a more peaceful state. It's no good suggesting that they just relax with soft music. They need to redirect their thoughts, so it is important that they have something to do. Besides, I believe it is important to take an active role in getting better. If they comply and really get into the spirit of things, they usually find that most of the niggly illnesses start to clear up, with no other changes being needed, save that of positive happy thoughts. Of course, I never recommend that anyone stop any medication that they may be taking. Similarly, if I suspect a person might need medical supervision, I would be the first to recommend it. I am not suggesting that serious illness can be cured by positive thought alone, because I know that, by the time it has reached the physical body, more help is needed. What I am saying is that it goes a long way to help, and is an excellent preventative of further illness. I know that constant negative thoughts and statements are very often the beginnings of illness just waiting for enough energy to gather together for it to manifest itself in the physical. The more you say or think a thing, the stronger the energy grows, as like attracts like.

I have a friend who never seems to get colds or flu viruses. When I ask him whether he has had that flu virus that is going around at the moment his reply is that he never get colds or flu. He hasn't got time for them. Yet everyone else is dropping like flies.

Past Life Experience

Past life experiences can be the cause of many illnesses. The trouble is that although reincarnation is a fascinating subject, and many people either believe in it, or feel that there may be something in it, it is still not regarded as even being a consideration when dealing with illness. Yet people develop illness seemingly out of the blue, without any logical explanation. Here is an example.

A young woman of twenty-eight years old suddenly develops

asthma. She doesn't know that she has always had a predisposition to asthma, not because it is 'in the family', but because it is in her energy field, and now it has manifested itself at a physical level. Suddenly at around the time of her twenty-eighth birthday, she starts getting asthma attacks. She doesn't smoke, nor does she work in a smoky atmosphere. She is happy in her work, not particularly stressed. She doesn't have any allergies or live near rape fields. She is not allergic to cats or dogs and has no particular food intolerance. Everyone is baffled. There seems no rhyme or reason for this sudden outbreak. In desperation the young woman seeks alternative medicine. Regressive hypnotherapy is suggested as the treatment. The young woman readily agrees. During the regression she experiences a past life where she is once again a young woman of about the age of twenty-eight. The scenario that follows for her could indeed be the memory of her past life, or it may be a past life experience that she has chosen, albeit unconsciously, from the collective unconscious (Akashic records) that parallels and represents her present life experiences. The experience may include a traumatic death such as suffocation, or being chased until she became so out of breath that her chest began to hurt and breathing became extremely difficult.

For the young woman just reaching the age of twenty-eight may be enough to trigger subconscious memories into action. This could be enough to trigger the physical manifestation in the form of an asthma attack. Being able to understand what may have happened to us in the past is often enough to stop an illness in its tracks. And someone like our young woman no longer suffers with asthma. It has gone as suddenly as it came. The power of the mind should never be underestimated.

Our Responsibility

Quite often people won't seek or accept help for a problem. Perhaps it is because of a fear of doctors, or the unknown, and what the problem may turn out to be. Perhaps they expect God to heal them, without any physical help or intervention, so they need not take any further action, save prayer. It maybe simply ignoring good advice, for example; 'Uncle Fred smoked like a trooper all his life, and lived to the age of ninety-four,' should not equal, 'So that's good enough for me'.

Then there is drug and alcohol abuse. All of these potential dangers and many others like them may seem obvious, but they are usually excuses that cover far more serious problems of a mental or emotional nature. It is our responsibility to look after our physical bodies, as well as our mental, emotional and spiritual bodies. It is up to us to confront our demons. In the same way it is important for us all to do our personal best as far as looking after our environment and ultimately our planet. We all have a responsibility to look after our planet. Our contributions may not seem very important or noticeable. However, collectively our efforts will make a significant difference, and that is extremely important. After all, our planet is also subject to the law of cause and effect and what we give out we will surely get back.

Collective and Group Energy

Another factor to consider is collective negative energy. You may work in an environment where all of your colleagues at work are very negative. Everyone may be dissatisfied with the conditions that they are working in. They may always be complaining, morale may be very low: too much load, for too few staff. As well as all of this, the staff will have their own personal problems that they have to deal with at home. When you enter such an environment, you naturally blend your energy field with those of your colleagues (we are constantly doing this wherever we go). Their negativity blends itself into your energy field. This adds to your personal negative feelings and increases your feelings of unhappiness, depression, anger or whatever. In a day or so this energy will dissipate and you will be more or less back to normal, save for your own bad feelings about your job. However because you have to go back into the fray on a day-to-day basis, you are constantly feeding your negativity. Not only with your own thoughts and feelings, but those of your colleagues also, which may be more bitter than your own. Although their energy may not stay with you for long, it is being renewed on a regular basis.

To be in a situation that makes you unhappy is one thing; you can control your thoughts and attitudes. But taking on board 'other people's stuff' is not so easy to deal with, because, of course, we cannot control other people's thoughts and feelings. But what it means to us is that feeling other people's negative energy makes it very difficult for us to rise above it. It's a bit like having a dark heavy blanket wrapped right around the office or work place. As this negativity gradually becomes engrained within your energy field, distortions start to appear. If you could see the energy field, in this state, it would look torn in places, with frayed edges, and the colours would be stained and muddy, perhaps even quite dark in places. As a spiritual healer I can feel these torn spots in a person's energy field. They feel very cold, as if air were escaping from something. At first this negative energy may only manifest itself as tiredness and stress, but eventually perhaps small niggly things start to go wrong with the physical body as the immune system starts to suffer. These, in turn, can lead to more serious illness.

Just before I close this chapter I would like to say that it is *never* a higher plan to induce illness, so that you can become an aid to medical research. Such would be a waste of life's opportunities. After all there are still enough people, who are creating enough illness, for research to be satiated.

Now that you have read these examples, you will be able to see how disease can develop and how important it is, yet again, for us to get better control of our thoughts and feelings.

Chapter Eleven
OCCULT

THE TWO LADIES FROM THE LOCAL CHURCH HAD CALLED ON one of their regular visits to our street. During our conversation, it became obvious to me that they were fascinated by the idea that I could consider Jesus, my mentor, and friend, and yet, I did not go to church, nor had any intention of joining one.

During their investigation to try and understand what made me tick, my interest in the tarot came out. Suddenly the ladies seemed really worried. The look on their faces was one of horror and concern. They hurriedly tried to advise me that I would be well advised to stay away from 'the occult', as it was evil and could do me harm. I tried, in my turn, to assure them, that I knew and understood the tarot very well. I told them that the word occult didn't mean evil. It means hidden, kept secret and, since I knew and understood the tarot very well, there was nothing to be afraid of. I then invited them in to inspect the cards. I would show them each one in turn and explain the cards to them, perhaps answer any questions they might have and, hopefully, give them a better insight. Then they would see for themselves that there was nothing to be afraid of. Instead of my offer being helpful, it set off alarm bells. They hurriedly made their excuses, and almost ran up the road, not stopping to knock at any one else's door. Feeling full of mischief, I couldn't help laughing, after I closed the front door. I remember thinking, that's a new one, I'll have to try that again, next time I'm in a hurry! But the reality of the situation was that these ladies were genuinely frightened and that is a very sorry state of affairs. So I thought it wouldn't hurt to include a chapter, on some of the famous 'Occult tools'.

As I have already mentioned, the word occult simply means, that which is hidden. It doesn't mean 'black magic', or evil practices, just hidden. However, it is generally associated with things of a psychic and paranormal nature. And unjustifiably, the psychic and paranormal are looked upon as being either wicked or a sign of mental instability, which is rather strange, since we are all naturally psychic, whether you wish to believe or not. It is just that some people have, shall we say, a more pronounced psychic ability than others.

One of the reasons that this is so, is that these people are not afraid to explore. They are open-minded. Fear and misguided beliefs will push your natural psychic abilities right down. Interestingly, I believe that, if we did not suppress our natural psychic abilities, our lives would be a whole lot easier, less painful and fearful. Yet over the centuries, we have seen fit to suppress a natural God-given gift! Anytime anything of a psychic nature that does occur is either passed off as one of those things: ignored, exorcised, taken to the doctor, or hushed up, for fear of ridicule. Even intuition is regularly ignored at our peril. Anyway let's see if we can clear up a few myths. Let's start with 'the dreaded tarot cards'.

Tarot cards go back thousands of years. If you've never seen a pack, let me describe them to you. There are seventy-eight cards in all, twenty-two major cards, and fifty-six minor cards. Let's start with the minor cards. If you pick up a set of ordinary playing cards, there are four jacks, four queens, four kings, four aces and numbered cards from two, to ten and there are four sets of these. These are clubs, spades, diamonds, and hearts. This is a modern set of playing cards, and what is left of the original tarot cards. Now all you need to do is add four cavaliers to the set, call the suits, rods, swords, coins, and cups and there you have a set of minor tarot cards. But don't discard the jester that comes with most modern packs, as you often do when playing a card game. He is important. The jester, or the fool, is one of the major tarot cards of which there are twenty-two; he is all that survives from the original tarot, in the modern pack.

In tarot packs the other twenty-one cards do survive, they are all picture cards, and are symbolic of life experiences. Yes the tower and death cards are there, but too many action movies have given them their sinister image. The death card is used mainly to represent the end of a situation and a new beginning in the pipeline. The tower shows that old ways are crumbling, maybe in a sudden and unexpected way, but not necessarily in a bad way. The cards themselves are just pictures on card; they have absolutely no power in them whatsoever. Any power given to them comes from you, the sitter, and the person who reads them for you. The cards are not magical, possessed by either good or evil spirits, or any other thing. They are just, as I said before, pictures on cards.

Some packs are very beautiful and richly decorated, whilst others in my opinion are quite horrible or plain. Like anything in life, choosing a pack is as personal as choosing wallpaper, or a picture to put up in your home. Some packs you will like, others you will not. However the artist designs them, the symbols remain basically the same. All packs have a fool, emperor, empress, sun, moon, stars. Whilst some packs are small and easy to handle, others are huge, and a bit awkward to shuffle.

But now let's get down to the interesting bit, 'the reading'. If you go for a reading, you may be ushered into a darkened room, steeped in mystery, with strange objects, and incense, or it could be just an ordinary room, at a kitchen table. The surroundings are largely immaterial. What matters, is the ability of the tarot reader, to read what is coming from you, the sitter. You two are now the power. You, the sitter, will be asked to shuffle the cards. Perhaps, you will be asked to ponder on what is troubling you, or what you are interested in. The reason for this is that your thoughts form within your auric energy field. Your aura contains energy of the past, present and the currently forming future. Note that I say currently forming future, because you have free will. Nothing is set in concrete. Therefore your destiny is largely in your own hands, to a greater or lesser degree. Also within your energy field are the links you have with other people in your life, along with the effects they may be having on your life. This isn't a bad time to point out that other people in your life also have free will. Therefore any tarot reading should be looked upon as a guide, rather than something that is set in concrete.

If you don't like the way a reading is panning out, remember that you can always take steps to change or minimise the effects. A good tarot reader will also be able to give good advice, help you to see other options. Anyone who leaves you feeling frightened, depressed or helpless, is very irresponsible. The cards that you choose from the pack, you choose with your own energy. You attract symbols from the pack, that best reflect your personal circumstances. Remember like attracts like.

Usually people go to a tarot reader because they either feel confused and unsure of their direction, or even afraid. Some may just go for a bit of a laugh. In my experience, most people have something on their mind, even if they don't want to admit it.

Sometimes people ask silly questions, like, 'Will I win the lottery?'

But their energy fields are loaded with their real concerns and the cards they choose will relate to these. Incidentally, I always ask the sitter to keep their questions to themselves, as I find it easier to read objectively, if I don't know in advance. This is true of many tarot readers.

Once your cards are chosen, the reader will lay out the cards in an arrangement preferable to him. There are many layouts. Some are created by the tarot reader himself, whilst others are time-honoured favourites. Most have a past, present and future theme, with any possible outcome. This is just a way for the reader to gain perspective. It isn't a magical rite that is performed when the cards are laid out, but some readers do like to include a sense of the dramatic. The important thing now is the skill of the reader, and the ability to interpret the symbolic images on the cards, individually and collectively.

Some readers will use the textbook meanings, others will read the cards intuitively. I personally use both. If the card reader is good, they will be able to tune into your energy field, and pick up, intuitively, or even clairvoyantly, the things that are going on, in and around you. But they are not mind readers as such. They don't know what you are thinking. But, because they are not usually emotionally involved with you, indeed they may never have met you before, they can usually see things more clearly than perhaps you can at that moment. A good tarot reader can be an invaluable help, and comfort when you may be feeling a bit lost.

Tarot cards are a tool. They assist the reader, by bringing visual images out into the open. A clairvoyant reader would not need this since they can actually see symbolic images in the aura of the sitter. More on that subject later.

The tarot has gained such a bad name, and causes many to be frightened by it. It's true purpose is to guide, help, assist and comfort. But there have been many irresponsible readers, who are both, at best naïve and inexperienced, whilst others enjoy the power trip, and can be manipulative, controlling, and greedy. They use fear to help feed their ego and pocket. Which is a shame, because the tarot, in the right hands, has a lot of good to offer.

If a tarot reader cannot seem to read your cards, it could mean that they are tired, or that you are too sceptical, and therefore, putting up a block. A responsible reader will be honest and tell you why they think that they cannot get a reading for you and not try to make things up, or leave you with the impression that, because they cannot 'see anything', you are about to die! A good reader will be sensitive to the fact that a lot of people are a little nervous of the unknown. If you do choose to see a tarot reader, go with a good recommendation from someone who's been before. Expect to pay a reasonable price for their time and skill, but steer clear of highly expensive readings. Don't forget to use your own intuition. That's what it's there for. Do you feel comfortable with the reader, are they warm and welcoming, or do you feel uncomfortable? Remember you can change your mind, you don't have to stay.

One final word; tarot readings are primarily there to put you in touch with yourself, to help and guide you. They may not be one hundred percent accurate, but that's where you come in. You really do know what's going on in your world better than anyone else. The tarot, and skills of the reader, are there to help you see more clearly and objectively. You can fill in the gaps.

Clairvoyance

A clairvoyant is someone who can see clearly. That is what the word means, and it has its origins in French. In fact, clairvoyance is just one way that these people work. Some people have more developed hearing. This is known as clairaudience, or clear hearing. Others sense and feel strongly. They are clairsentient.

Clairvoyance is a popular term used to describe anyone who sees into the future, but a lot of clairvoyants are capable of one or all of the other faculties. Some are more developed than others. Some clairvoyants use tools to assist them. These are such things as the tarot, as we have already discussed, crystal balls, rune stones, pendulums and many other tools. Whatever they feel a personal affinity with. Others don't need anything at all. I have a friend who is clairvoyant, clairaudient and clairsentient and who is also mediumistic. She will often start a reading with tarot cards, but once she is in tune, she doesn't need them. She stops looking at them, and just chats on, as she picks up symbols, hears voices and feels emotions. Clairvoyance is simply the ability to tap into your energy field, and read you via the thought forms that have formed in your energy field from the past, present and the future that you are currently creating, or that you are predestined to experience.

Other people's energy also surrounds you, either by recent contact, or by the thoughts and feelings you have for each other. Just as your thoughts travel to someone else, (whether you want them to or not) their thoughts and feelings travel back to you and filtrate your energy field. You have a constant stream of energy flowing between you and those with whom you are intimate, be it a pleasant or unpleasant intimacy. This is known as a karmic bond. Your energy field isn't a constant height and size. It changes as your consciousness expands outwards toward someone else, either consciously or subconsciously. We are constantly interconnecting with each other. This is why it is possible for a clairvoyant to be able to pick up thoughts and feelings and possible actions, reactions, and intentions that another person in your life may have with regard to you, and the situation you may both share.

Clairvoyants can see what we are attracting to ourselves, such as opportunities, new jobs, relationships, potential illness. We are constantly creating and attracting, and a clairvoyant can see and interpret the energy that is currently in our energy field. I realise that this is only a brief description of clairvoyance, but I hope you are beginning to see that these people are not mad, wicked or working with the devil. They don't cast spells, or try to make you do things against your will. The power comes from you and your willingness to open up and let the clairvoyant see clearly. They are just using a natural gift that we all have the potential to use. Of course some are more naturally developed than others. As with all things in life there are those who will use the gift more negatively, inappropriately or misguidedly, but most clairvoyants, will not tune into you on a too personal level unless you ask them to. They can't see your every thought. However some are so sensitive that it is not unusual for them to pick up things about you in what seems like a spontaneous way. This is especially so if you are going through a pretty intense experience at any particular time.

An example is when you walk into a room. Your hosts are laughing and smiling as they greet you, and yet you can feel the atmosphere, without having any prior knowledge. You know that your hosts have been having an argument with each other. You don't know how you know, but you can feel it. You are using your intuition, you are being clairsentient. A clairvoyant can see it. The intensity of the argument means that the energy is still strong, thought forms still linger on the ether and in your energy field. Therefore they cannot help but see. If they are discreet they won't say anything. People are afraid of clairvoyants, but they needn't be. We are all naturally clairvoyant. It's just that in general we haven't developed our sixth sense much yet. But we all will in time. When we leave our physical bodies, and take up residence in the spirit world again, we will become exceptionally clairvoyant, audient and sentient. It's what we are, conscious energy.

Mediums

Mediums have gained a very bad reputation, due to fakes and people who like to elaborate and sensationalise. Mediums are associated with the dead, ghosts and spirit guides, ectoplasm, heavy breathing, strange voices, fainting, poltergeists, trances, and messages from the dead that turn out to be nothing but mumbo jumbo. No wonder mediums get such a bad press. Of course there are those who like to be dramatic and give a wonderful exhibition, worthy of an Oscar, everyday of the week. Unfortunately this kind of behaviour denigrates a gift that has been given to help those who are grieving, or confused about life after death.

Having said that, being a medium is not just about life after death and relaying messages of comfort and hope. Many mediums relay messages of spiritual guidance from the spirit world and from the sitter's spiritual guides. There are two types of medium as far as I am aware. These are trance mediums and clairvoyant mediums.

Let's start with the clairvoyant type. This is the type of gift which my friend has. Like most mediums of this type, she combines her skills of clairvoyance and mediumistic abilities to have private sittings with someone. In this way she is able to give a reading for the sitter, which includes their own life, past, present and future and also receive any messages from the spirit world from a loved one who has died. Their work is in the main to help, comfort and give hope and new direction. Most mediums are genuine, warm, loving, compassionate people, but their skill may be vastly variable in levels of development. A medium cannot summon up the dead, or make them talk to you. If your dearly departed doesn't want to talk to you, for whatever reason, a medium cannot disturb them. A medium is just a channel, who relays messages that they receive and which may be in the form of symbols, or scenarios that are played out. Or they maybe actual messages of speech variety, or intense feelings, according to the medium's abilities.

What needs to be understood, is that, just as a medium has to learn and develop the skill of channelling, a person in spirit also has to learn how to relay messages and will gravitate toward a medium with whom they feel comfortable, and can work with. This is why, sometimes, in the early days of losing a loved one and going to see a medium, the reading can be somewhat unsatisfactory. Your loved one may not have found the right medium to work with. They may be desperate to get a message to you and will try any medium who is available to begin with. Later when they become more skilled, they not only choose a good medium to work with, but will be skilful in leading you to the medium of their choice. Then they can blend their consciousness with that of the medium who can then relay their thoughts and feelings to you via the medium's clairvoyant skills. A loved one will make use of all of the skills that the medium has to offer, in order to put a point across to you. The medium has to interpret many symbols, phonetic sounds and feelings. In fact it is nothing short of a miracle! But it is largely down to the loving people, who are known as mediums, who have the courage to continue developing their natural gifts despite the bad press and ridicule that they attract.

People often ask, why can my loved one speak to a medium, but they never speak to me? This question has already been mostly answered. It is not that our loved ones don't want to speak to us, you can be sure that they do try to get through to you, especially when they first die. But, when a soul leaves the physical world, they move on to a world of higher vibrations. They have to learn how to slow down their vibrations as much as they can, but they cannot slow down enough to reach us. It is up to us to reach up to them. By this I mean, we have to quieten our minds, become calm, and tranquil, relaxed and positive. Clear out the clutter of our everyday, materialistic minds and think of our loved ones. Then we are more likely to reach them and they will be able to get through to us. Also it takes a bit of getting used to, this new telepathic and symbolic language. We need to let go of the idea of ordinary speech.

Most of us find this sort of thing difficult and we tend to have blocks; being overwrought with emotion when we think of our loved ones. Or perhaps caused by fear, or scepticism about survival after death. Perhaps we have been brought up to believe that it is wrong to want to speak to our loved ones, once they have gone to the spirit world. A lot of religions teach that the dead sleep till judgement day. Whatever the reason, we put up a lot of barriers, and yet, we are potentially mediumistic. We have access to both a logical and an intuitive mind, but we still seem to favour the logical mind and dismiss the intuitive mind. Therefore we could regularly be missing signals from our loved ones that are saying that they are trying to contact you, please listen! So we dismiss any thoughts or feelings we may be getting, as just imagination. That is why we have to rely on mediums to channel messages for us. Of course, some mediums will be better than others and so they have to train their natural gift until it is better developed and disciplined. However, one day, we will drop all our barriers. As we evolve and relearn how to get in touch with our intuitive minds, we will find that there will be more and more natural mediums. And, as they will not have to learn how to get in touch with their intuitive minds, they will be able to contact their loved ones naturally themselves.

Trance Mediums

Trance mediums are the most famous type of medium. The ones of Victorian parlour fame, the ones that are most frequently portrayed in films and on television. I don't claim to know a lot about trance mediums. I have never seen one in action. But apparently the medium quietens the mind, becomes relaxed, and allows a spirit person, often someone who claims to be the medium's spirit guide, to come into the body, and use it as an instrument of communication. In this way a guide can speak to a large group of people at a time, if they have an important message to convey. Apparently it is not unusual for the medium's physical features to change somewhat, or for the voice to change. For instance a male spirit guide may use the body of a female medium and the voice may deepen. But if the woman has a natural soprano voice, then the change will be restricted to this range level of the physical vehicle. Apparently during the time that the spirit person occupies the body, the medium's mind astral-travels to a place of quiet rest somewhere in the spirit world. Just as a medium cannot force a spirit person to come and speak to them, neither can spirit people force a medium to let them borrow their body for a short while. It has to be by mutual consent and at a higher level. This is such hard work for both medium and spirit person that messages are given in short time periods. Often the medium will come out of trance for a rest, before re-entering a trance again. Often the medium will have no recollection of what has been said and relies very much on tape recordings and other people's accounts. Whilst I have no doubt at all that such mediumistic ability is possible, I would have to question the level of guidance that comes through, as it would be just as easy for a self-important spirit person to come through to give guidance. But, as I have never been to see a trance medium in action, I would have to reserve judgement. I'm sure there are many channels for true spiritual guidance. It's just that I like to test things very thoroughly first. This is down to the training I received from my teacher.

Edgar Cayce is a fine example of a trance medium who did a lot of wonderful work to help many people during his lifetime. He was also known as the sleeping prophet. There are many books written about his experiences available should you wish to read about him.

Ouija Board

Or planchette as it is sometimes called. Now this is one I would not recommend to most people. It's not that it is evil or black magic, or anything like that, but in the wrong hands, or should I say in the wrong minds, it can have devastating effects. If you know what you are doing, it can be used sensibly. I understand how it works, but I would still be reluctant to take part, because you are not just relying on your mind, but a group of minds. However I believe that you can buy a planchette in some countries as a child's game. I've never seen one on sale in this country.

However, it is very easy to make your own. All you need are some flat pieces of card, each with a letter of the alphabet on them, and a blank card. Also, you need a card with yes, and another with no, written on it, and a small glass. The alphabet letters are placed in a circle, the blank card between Z and A with the yes and no cards in the centre at each end, and the glass upturned in the centre. Now all you need are several participants. Each person sits around the circle and each person places a finger, usually the little finger, as this is less easy to force than the index finger, on the upturned glass.

The session usually begins with some kind of prayer, asking for protection and guidance, and then the speaker for the group will ask if there is anyone there who would like to speak to anyone in the group. After a period of quiet, when everyone in the group is supposed to concentrate as one, the glass will start to move, seemingly of its own accord. In actual fact this is being achieved by mind energy, known as telekinesis. Whether the mind is from a departed spirit, or from one or more members of the group, is difficult to say at this stage. However, words are usually spelled out as the glass travels from letter to letter to form a message, either for the group as a whole, or for one of the members of the group. This is a laborious process, but it can get results. A spirit person will use any form of communication, in order to get a message across to someone, no matter how crude the system. So far so good, if you know and understand what is happening and nobody in the group is of a nervous disposition. Then all well and good. Many people have regular sessions and good experiences if they behave in a positive and sensible way.

Now, herein lies the key. They approach it in the right frame of mind. By now you may have worked things out. All of these things, be they cards, runes, pendulums, or ouija, all rely on mind energy. Only, with the Ouija, usually a group of minds come together. Now, everybody in the group may look as if they are feeling confident, but it only takes one frightened mind in the group, or even a mind that is angry and still churned up about something that happened to them that day, to bring the level of consciousness down to a lower level. So now, when you begin, you will attract spirit from a lower level of consciousness. Quite often, everyone in the group is operating at their own level. The group are not always 'as one'. This is when people are likely to have a bad experience, and can run into serious trouble, as you are tampering with mind energy, and it is very, very powerful. When everybody in the group is working together, their like minds will attract like-minded spirits and they can receive uplifting messages, sometimes from loved ones, at other times, from strangers.

When the group are operating at a lower level, or different levels, they will attract spirits of a lower level of consciousness through the strongest emotions, which are often fear. At this level of consciousness, you can attract what is known as elemental spirits, who are so twisted and distorted with negative thought, that their projection of outward appearance is ugly and grotesque. They feed on the fear of others and have a distorted pleasure in someone else's fear and misery. If you attract this level, the energy becomes forceful. As you add your thoughts of fear to that of the

142

spirit entity, you could very well start experiencing poltergeist activity, such as the glass shooting across the table. Even the table could be turned upside down and ornaments smashed. At times these spirits use bad language, they give threatening and frightening messages. Inexperienced sitters usually don't know how to dismiss these spirits and often leave the circle before a proper cleansing and clearing can take place. Because these elemental spirits feed on fear, they attach themselves to the most frightened member of the group by entering that person's auric energy field, who can then become plagued by nightmares or become depressed, even suicidal. They may start hearing voices that are full of profanities, both threatening and frightening. The person could become cajoled, and influenced by the entity to do things that are out of character.

The idea of the entity is to enjoy watching the person destroy himself or herself. If a person's mind is weak, this experience could go on indefinitely. If a person is stronger, they may get away with just a few nightmares. I realise I am showing the worse scenario here, but it can, and unfortunately, does happen. A milder case scenario would be that of the group being led up the garden path. You can attract a spirit, who likes to play mischief, or, who is full of self-importance, and sees themselves as a spirit guide who comes to give you so-called important guidance, or messages. If you are not on the ball, you could easily be impressed, or flattered, and let yourself be guided into all sorts of trouble. Or somewhere that gets you nowhere, which can be just as bad, since you are being led away from your true spiritual goals. Such messages on closer examination will almost undoubtedly prove to be a load of rubbish. Then, of course, you may not attract spirit at all, but can end up talking among your fellow group members, bringing up unconscious thoughts and feelings, passing on messages or making up gobbledegook. You will not necessarily be aware of this and may think that a spirit person is responsible for the messages. Your experience very much depends on the level of consciousness of the whole group and what is being sent out, in other words: fear, arrogance, peace or tranquillity. Like attracts like, but it takes experience and sincerity to attract a higher level of consciousness than the individuals among the group. It is rare to attract anything higher than the highest level of consciousness in the group, even if they are strong and focused. But a focused group, on a high level, may attract true spiritual guidance, as group energy is stronger than individual energy. Whilst I think it is possible to achieve this I would generally advise to err on the side of caution where any spiritual guidance is concerned. I have mainly concentrated on the negative side of the ouija, mostly because I know how powerful the mind is, and when negative and concentrated thoughts combine, albeit unintentionally, as in a group, it is truly potentially dangerous.

Having said that, in its favour, it is possible to receive genuine messages of love, hope and encouragement from spirit people, departed relatives and loved ones, or just caring souls who want to help. It is possible to be asked a favour or request, as my husband experienced, when he was in his late teens. Here is his story of Frederick Cannon.

Frederick Cannon

My husband and a few friends had tried seances on a few occasions. They were always very careful to take safeguards and show respect for the forces that they were facing. Mostly there was little meaningful response. But on one occasion a character called Frederick Cannon made himself known. Over a number of sessions he would appear every time and gradually certain details unfolded.

Basically he claimed he was unable to rest because he wanted a Christian burial. His story was that the railways were pushing through the new line into the West Country. A number of the local inhabitants owned land and were refusing to sell. As a violent warning to the others, Frederick, his wife and two children were killed and their bodies thrown down an old mineshaft.

My husband lived in Nailsea, in Somerset, an area with an industrial past. There had been a thriving glass industry based on local coal. There were a number of disused shafts in the area. The railway ran south-west, nearer to Backwell, an adjoining village. Assuming the railway was put through in about the 1840s or 1850s this tied in with the demise of the local pits.

Frederick continued to insist he wanted a Christian burial. So my husband and his friends decided that they would give him one. The problem was which mineshaft had been selected for the disposal of the bodies? They came up with the idea of a portable ouija board. Having 'discussed' the plan with Fred, they set off one day into the countryside with a large book (the board) and a tin lid (the glass) asking questions as they went, 'Is this the way?' – clockwise movement for yes, anti-clockwise for no. By this rudimentary system they arrived, incredibly, at a mineshaft about two miles away. By no means the nearest, but interestingly one of the nearest shafts to the railway line and Backwell.

So the group stood quietly and respectfully and read the funeral service from the prayer book, with which they had come equipped. Fredrick had promised he would show his thanks and, amazingly, on the way back money was found in a pocket which allegedly was not there before. (Material manifestations such as money are known as apports.)

More interestingly, there was only ever one more 'meeting' with Fred who gave his thanks and never came again, in spite of a series of seances. He was at peace.

Was this just a mischief-maker, or a soul in desperate need of help? We shall never know. It did however leave a lasting impression on the group.

I should say here that a Christian burial is not a requirement for entry into the spirit world. However, if you believe strongly enough that it is, then it would be enough to keep you stuck on the etheric plane if you did not get a Christian burial. On this occasion I would have to say that the Ouija had a good purpose, as it was instrumental in assisting what I would term as rescue work.

Chapter Twelve

FINALLY

A S OUR LITTLE SOJOURN BETWEEN THE SPIRIT AND PHYSICAL worlds comes to a close, I hope that you have found it as fascinating as I have to write it, and that some of your questions have been answered. If it has left you with even more questions – that's good. The more questions we ask, with a sincere desire to know, the more we will grow and evolve spiritually.

My husband says, 'It's easy for me to get answers, because I have a hot line to God.'

I have to say answers don't always come easily, but I do talk to God a lot. I ask him all sorts of things, I know I will be answered, but sometimes I have to wait for the answer. At times I have to work hard for an answer, whilst others come instantly, but I always get an answer. We all have a hot line to God. You just have to get plugged in. You don't have to go to a church to talk to God; neither do you have to kneel by your bedside, so long as you have privacy. Just open your heart and chat. Believe in what you are doing and know you will get an answer. God may have put the answer machine on for a while, unless your prayer is urgent, but he will get back to you. Don't expect a thunder bolt, or angels, (well, you never know, so don't rule it out all together) but answers come in different ways. I find absolutely fascinating the many different ways that my prayers have been answered. The more you talk to God, the easier it gets.

You are a very powerful being, a co-creator with God. Hopefully you have realised just how powerful, not only is your mind, but how powerful that makes you. Think of it this way. Can you really afford to think half of the things that you might have been used to thinking? If you want to change your world, change your mind. *You* have the power to do it.

Before I finish, I would like to offer you my sincere and best wishes for your future happiness, and leave you with this lovely poem.

The Golden Gate

Love is by far the most important thing of all. It is the Golden Gate of Paradise. Pray for the understanding of Love, and meditate upon it daily. It casts out fear; it is fulfilling of the Law. It covers a multitude of sins. Love is absolutely invincible.

There is no difficulty that enough Love will not conquer, no disease that enough Love will not heal; no door that enough Love will not open; no gulf that enough Love will not bridge; no wall that enough Love will not throw down; no sin that enough Love will not redeem.

It makes no difference how deeply seated may be the trouble, how hopeless the outlook, how muddled the tangle, how great the mistake; a sufficient realisation of Love will dissolve it all. If only you could Love enough you would be the happiest and most powerful being in the world.

Emmet Fox

Remember that to every question, the answer is always *love*; remember also that there are Many Facets of Love.

Recommended Reading

Life in the World Unseen by Anthony Borgia (sadly out of print, but second hand book shops will often conduct a search for you)

Embraced by the Light by Betty J Edie. Aquarian Press (an imprint of Harper Collins publishers)

Testimony of Light by Helen Greaves, published by C.W. Daniel Co Ltd

The Power of Positive Thinking by Norman Vincent Peale. Published by Cedar (an imprint of Reed Consumer Books Ltd)

In Tune with the Infinite by Ralph Waldo Trine. Published by Mandala (an imprint of Harper Collins publishers)

Bring out the Magic in your Mind by Al Koran. Published by Thorson (an imprint of Harper Collins publishers)

Your Heart's Desire by Sonia Choquette. Piatkus Publishers Ltd

Printed in the United Kingdom
by Lightning Source UK Ltd.
101230UKS00001B/169-186